PEACE PLAYS

THE TRAGEDY OF KING REAL
by
Adrian Mitchell

THE CELEBRATION OF KOKURA
by
Berta Freistadt

CLAM
by
Deborah Levy

KEEPING BODY AND SOUL TOGETHER
by
Stephen Lowe

THE FENCE
by
Common Ground

Selected and introduced by
Stephen Lowe

A METHUEN PAPERBACK

First published in Great Britain as a Methuen Paperback original in 1985 by
Methuen London Ltd, 11 New Fetter Lane, London EC4P 4EE
and in the United States of America by Methuen Inc, 29 West 35th Street, New York,
NY 10001.

Set in IBM 10pt Press Roman by 🅐 Tek-Art
Reproduced, printed and bound in Great Britain by
Hazell Watson & Viney Limited,
Member of the BPCC Group,
Aylesbury, Bucks

British Library Cataloguing in Publication Data

Peace Plays. — (A Methuen theatrefile)
    1. English drama — 20th century
    I. Lowe, Stephen, *1947-*
822'.914'08   PR1272

ISBN 0-413-56000-7

CAUTION
All rights whatsoever in these plays are strictly reserved and applications for
performance, readings etc, must be made before rehearsals begin to the authors or
their agents, as follows:

The Tragedy of King Real: Fraser & Dunlop (Scripts) Ltd, 91 Regent Street, London
    W1R 8RU
The Celebration of Kokura: Berta Freistadt, 5a Oxford Gardens, London W10
Clam: Deborah Levy, 121 Clissold Crescent, London N16
Keeping Body and Soul Together: Goodwin Associates, 12 Rabbit Row, London
    W8 4DX
The Fence: Common Ground, Peat Meadow Farmhouse, Off Derby Road, Risley,
    Draycott, Derby DE7 3SS

CONTENTS

INTRODUCTION

The Theatre of Peace

On Whitehall, there is a theatre with a famous history. It was once the home of 'British Farce', but some years back the curtain fell on its vicars with their falling trousers for the last time. It rose again to reveal women in even greater states of undress, who in turn were sacrificed on the altar of greed to make way for the real money spinner — a theatre that now proudly bears the name of 'The Theatre of War'.

In October 1983, I was on the part of that giant CND march which passed this theatre on its way to Hyde Park. On top of the building opposite was a small group of clowns (not, I suspect, subsidised by the Arts Council but by an even more secret organisation) blasting out the theme songs of anti-red hatred, and trying to sell their mindless brand of patriotism that can only comprehend a national identity by violent opposition to another.

But I can't deny they affected me. Wedged in between those two theatres of war with the whole dead weight of the rest of Whitehall supporting them, I found myself suddenly unable to move, as despair at their killing stupidity struck me. I didn't know what to do. When that panic hits you like the SAS what do you do? It's difficult sometimes just to keep breathing, never mind discover a positive action.

I think I might have just frozen there, if it wasn't for the mass movement around me that I'd forgotten, who gently took me and my child along with it. And as I moved on, I saw the march as the helicopter cameras might have seen it, as a vast dragon of anger and hope, weaving its way through the sharp edges of the streets of London, like the dragon that had surrounded the camp at Greenham a few months before. And I felt we had all become a living example of 'The Theatre of Peace'.

Of course it's easy to bandy the word PEACE around. The producers of the arms industry employ it all the time, and even given they can only find B-movie actors or elocution trained dummies to mouth their speeches, still their definition of the word comes across loud and clear. Peace, under our present leaders, is a sterile state of passivity, where the people are to flinch from every cloud in the fear that in its belly it carries worse than raindrops to fall upon our heads. Peace in their mouths is as trapped as the word love in a porno movie. It's time to release it, before they make not only it, but all of us, totally perverted, if not ultimately impotent.

The dictionaries categorise Peace only as a noun, a static state, a period of absence — 'Peace is freedom *from* or cessation *of* war'. War, interestingly, is both a noun and a verb. It is an activity. Something one can do.

All this makes Peace sound as exciting as a Sunday run by the Lord's Day Observance Society, and I, for one, am not campaigning for that. But things liven up considerably if we check back on the word's derivation. Peace, it transpires, is, 'cognate with pangere, pact — to fix'. So, apparently, it was once seen as an active state. Once upon a time, it was once understood differently. There is a verb fighting to get out of there. And of course, of late, many people have come to realise this, have begun to claim Peace for the entire week, as their place of work, as their very state of being.

Such a radical stance brings a certain traditional reaction. In the theatre, as elsewhere, we can see it well enough, from the efforts by Education Ministers and others to block Peace Plays in schools through to the Minister of Defence's attempts to close down the highly successful run at the Greenham Common Theatre. And in addition to this, of course, they are engaged in a mass campaign of promotion to sell us their Theatre of War. It's a farce, true, but as all pros know, farce is a deadly serious business, and none more so than this, for if things go bad, and it 'bombs' we may end up rolling uncontrollably in the aisles but it won't be through a fit of laughter.

We are now engaged in a greater debate than just saying NO to nuclear weapons, and there is a central obligation to articulate and affirm a radically different concept of life. For that to be possible we have to not only understand more deeply the causes that have brought us to this eleventh hour but also the essential aspirations and desires that might lead us creatively beyond it. And in this I believe the theatre can play a very significant part, and it's a part it is beginning to respond to in an exciting fashion.

The last few years have seen a remarkable growth in the number of peace plays and also a new audience prepared to risk often appalling theatrical conditions to see them. The Peace Play Register (published by the Theatre Writers Union) lists over three hundred plays of all shapes and sizes and this number is increasing daily. Having read a good selection of them, I fear most would not satisfy the National critic who last year bemoaned the absence of the 'Great Peace Play'. Whilst in no way wishing to deprive him of this splendid work, I worry that if we all frown and search diligently for the proverbial four leafed clover, we could fail to step back and marvel at the sheer breadth of ground covered by the bank of clover. There is something final about the notion of the 'Great Peace Play' and if there's something we can all agree on, Final Solutions are to be opposed. Let us all beware the day the Evening Standard offers an award for the 'Best Peace Play'.

Certain types of Peace Plays do, of course, get published. Largely those associated with the type of work done at the Royal Court, the National Theatre or the RSC, but there is as yet no volume that begins to show the wider scope of the work, going on in schools, studios, in street festivals, or at the very fence of Greenham itself. That has been a key factor in my selection of these pieces.

If any of you feel that all Peace Plays are grey depressing sagas set in nuclear bunkers (the sort of play to which you might lend your moral support but not your physical presence) then you might find the diversity of response here surprising. Although I suspect the starting point of these plays is all FEAR, it is not a fear that wishes to hide itself away, and it draws its strength from that human characteristic that William Faulkner aptly defines as 'I decline to accept the end of man.' And now we must clearly add woman. (Even more clearly in the light of the fact that the large majority of the playwrights in this volume are women).

I hope the range of these plays will take your breath away, and perhaps even inspire you to consider the theatre language as part of your work for Peace. For the Theatre of Peace, be that Greenham, or Greenpeace, or the local rep company, has the language to discover images of truth that the impressarios of the Theatre of War want suppressed.

But we mustn't be conned into thinking Peace is merely an 'issue' and that 1983, or any other year, was its year. Peace is not an issue but an active verb. And the Theatre of Peace is something we all should be involved in, if we are going to peace together a future.

Otherwise there won't be one. The curtain will have fallen.

Clearly the problem is so fundamental that it now stands as a challenge to us all as creative beings to dream and bring into shape a world that does not yet exist. As Gabriel Garcia Marquez's wrote in his speech to the Nobel Peace Foundation:

Faced with this awesome reality that must have seemed a mere utopia through all of human time, we, the inventors of tales, who will believe anything, feel entitled to believe that it is not yet too late to engage in the creation of a utopia of a very different kind. A new and sweeping utopia of life, where no one will be able to decide for others how they die, where love will prove true and happiness be possible, and where the races condemned to one hundred years of solitude will have, at last and forever, a second opportunity on earth. (Transl. from the Spanish by Marina Castaneda.)

One last thought: it's amazing how clover can take over even the most well controlled lawn, isn't it?

Stephen Lowe
London 1985

P.S. Since writing this introduction the public 'Theatre of War' on Whitehall has been closed down. No doubt it is still going on underground there, but it is still a heartening indication of a healthy change.

THE TRAGEDY
OF
KING REAL

Adrian Mitchell is a poet, playwright and novelist. His original stage shows include *Tyger, Man Friday, Mind Your Head, White Suit Blues, A Seventh Man, In the Unlikely Event of an Emergency* and *The Hoagy, Bix and Wolfgang Beethoven Bunkhaus.* He also wrote the libretto for Peter Schat's circus opera *Houdini.* For Welfare State International he wrote *Uppandown Mooney* and *King Real and the Hoodlums* (and also contributed songs to their *Raising the Titanic*). In addition, he has written extensively for children's theatre and for television and has published four novels and six books of poems and given more than 1,000 performances of his poems. Most recently he wrote the lyrics for Peter Hall's adaptation of *Animal Farm,* and a new version of Calderon's *The Great Theatre of the World.* His adaptation of foreign plays include *Marat/Sade, The Mayor of Zalamea* and *The Government Inspector* (National Theatre) and *Life's a Dream* (RSC with John Barton).

The Tragedy of King Real was commissioned by Welfare State International, who are my favourite dramatic group on this planet. They are such a practical, visionary group that I had no hesitation in asking them to design and enact a nuclear war. They did so, in a movie called *King Real and the Hoodlums* which is based on this script and filmed in Barrow with a cast drawn from that strange Trident town. The play is dedicated to all that Company.

It is possible to produce this play either in a theatre or outdoors.

It must be performed with Pete Moser's music, which is adaptable to any size of band.

The design should not be realistic but must be astonishing.

King Lear is the greatest piece of writing in the English language and I have used its story and many of its beautiful lines because I needed them. I also used Tom O'Bedlam songs, songs by Thomas Durfey and Anon. I would like to thank these collaborators.

The end of the play brings not a happy ending but an alternative beginning. Doomsday is more than likely but not inevitable.

Adrian Mitchell
1984

The film, *King Real and the Hoodlums* was made in 1983 by Welfare State International in association with Sheffield Poly and was directed by John Fox and Paul Hayward.

The music for the songs in this play will be found at the end of the text. The songs from the play are also available on tape from Welfare State International, PO Box 9, Ulverston, Cumbria.

Characters
LORD THOMAS THE THOMAS, a musician, later POOR TOM
THE ARCHBISHOP OF STARE, later SURGEON TO THE STATE
KING REAL, King of Angaland
RAYGAL, his daughter, Princess of the North
GONILLA, his daughter, Princess of the South
CLOUDELLA, his daughter, Princess of the Sky, later CLOWN
CAPTAIN ADDERMAN, an army captain, later a GENERAL
HOTPOINT, a penguin, assistant and familiar to Raygal
ENOCH, a monkey, assistant and familiar to Gonilla
RAINDOG, Cloudella's dog, woolly and ginger
WAGTAIL/SPEAKER OR SINGER

Scenes
One: The Palace Gardens
Two: The Road to the Wasteland
Three: The Royal Bunker
Four: The Cold Wasteland
Five: The Royal Bunker
Six: The Hot Wasteland
Seven: The Royal Bunker

Scene One

The Palace gardens.
Beautiful gardens. Multi-coloured flowers. Fine trees. A throne of flame-coloured flowers. But not visible yet.
LORD THOMAS THE THOMAS, *a hip but out-of-date musician enters, instrument in hand. He speaks with musical accompliment. Intense spot on him. No other light.*

LORD THOMAS: I saw a vision on my
    vision machine
  I saw a vision but what did it mean?
  Vision of puppets playing power
    games
  Vision of the world like a flower in
    flames
  Pain of the planet beating in my head
  Pain of the planet till the planet went
    dead.
  I saw a vision on my vision machine
  I saw a vision but what did it mean?
  I wish I knew
  I wish I knew
  I wish I knew.

Lights full up – LORD THOMAS
relaxes.

Lord Thomas the Thomas is what they
  call me –
Leader of the jivin' aristocracy.
Got a vice-like grip and a loose upper
  lip
And I wanna put you hip to this
  tragedy trip.

He blows a horn in a wild, brief solo.

There once was a king and he had
  three daughters
And a nuclear shelter as snug as a
  tortoise.
His daughters were the crunchiest
  from coast to coast,
They carried the aroma of hot
  buttered toast –
But – he wondered which one of them
  loved him most.
So he announced a kind of freaky
  audition –
A Who Loves The King Most
Competition.

The results of this contest we'll now
  reveal
As we play *The Tragedy of King Real!*

Fanfare.

Now about some cats you must've
  heard it said!
That boy got eyes in the back of his
  head.
Well, meet a super-spook with eyes
  everywhere!
Chaplain to the king – The
  Archbishop of Stare.

Bluesy music, real churchy.
Enter the ARCHBISHOP OF STARE. His robes and mitre are covered with eyes, very like a peacock.

ARCHBISHOP (*intones*): There are some
  sinners whose mouths stink of
  death –
  O dearly beloved brethren and sistren,
  Have you ever wondered about bad
    breath?
  Come, sanctify your oral orifice with
    Listerine!

LORD THOMAS: That thought's reet
  sweet, My Lord of Stare,
  I can see the punters are highly
    impressed,
  But don't you think we ought to sort
    of prepare
  For King Real's Famous Love
    Contest?

Drum roll. Fanfare.

ARCHBISHOP: Too late, I can tell, by
  that prrum-prum-drumming
  And zippeday fanfare – the King is
    coming.
  Ladies etcetera – King Real!

As KING REAL approaches his throne, nodding to the humble populace, ARCHBISHOP, LORD THOMAS and MUSICIANS sing.

King Real
Rules the land and the sea.
King Real
To the power of three.
King Real King Real

You'd better get your knees in training
   to kneel
And practise crawling on your belly
   like an eel
Or he'll run you over in his
   royalmobile
King Real — that Real King — King
   Real.

King Real
All victorious
King Real
Ultra-glorious
King Real King Real
When he marches into battle hear his
   enemies squeal
For he smashes them and bashes
   them from head to heel
With cast-iron clobberers and slicers of
   steel
King Real — that Real King — King
   Real.

King Real
Real as real estate
King Real King Real
Real
As the wheel of fate
King Real King Real
He generously tells us what to think
   and feel
For a king must be king like a bell has
   to peal
And he knows the common man's a
   bloody imbecile
King Real — that Real Real Real Real
   Real Real King — King Real!

KING REAL, *a jovial but steely king,
takes his throne. White beard; white
hair; red face; posh clothes, including a
robe worn over the jacket of his suit.*

KING REAL: There's a clock in my head.
   I hear it chime!
Wintertime, wintertime, wintertime.
And wintertime seems like a good
   hour
To give up the three Great Keys of
   Power.
   The Great Key of Silver
   The Great Key of Gold
   And, greatest, the Key of Holy
     Crystal.

The ARCHBISHOP *produces each key
as it is named.*

ARCHBISHOP: Abdication? What a
   brave, generous,
Selfless example to all of us!

LORD THOMAS: But how can *we*
   abdicate, your Grace?
We got no crowns in the first place!

ARCHBISHOP. I speak in metaphores.

LORD THOMAS: I read you.

ARCHBISHOP: Your Majesty, who shall
   succeed you?
KING REAL: I have three daughters.
   Each shall win one key.
   Call them. Put them to the test.
   Let each declare how much she loves me.
   The Crystal Key's for she who loves
     me best.
   Lord Thomas of Thomas, call my
     first-born forth.

LORD THOMAS: Raygal, the Princess of
   the North.

RAYGAL *appears on an iceberg,
accompanied by her familiar — a
penguin called* HOTPOINT.
RAYGAL's *colours are white and
silver and purple and black.*

RAYGAL (*sings*): The polar bear's white
   fury as he kills
The terror of the hunter as his kayak
   overturns
The endlessness of landscapes of white
   deserts and white hills
The monstrous Himalayas where the
   Yeti yearns
That's how I love you
Wild as a blizzard
That's how I love you
Big as a blizzard
That's how I love you
Blind, blind, blind,
Blind as a blizzard.

Explorers trudging forward on
   blackened toes
And glaciers that crawl along with
   mighty sighs
The albatross that flickers purple
   shadows on the snows

Eternal gazing of the north's white
eyes
That's how I love you
Wild as a blizzard
That's how I love you
Big as a blizzard
That's how I love you
Blind, blind, blind,
Blind as a blizzard.

KING REAL: Raygal, my daughter, you
shall be
Queen in the Power of the Silver Key.

The ARCHBISHOP *presents the silver key to* RAYGAL, *who becomes a queen there and then. A crown appears on her head, robes round her shoulders. Silver rain.* ALL *applaud.* RAYGAL *embraces* KING REAL, *with pecks on the cheek, like an actress who has to kiss a tycoon.*

KING REAL: Lord Thomas, employ
your mighty mouth
To call Gonilla —

LORD THOMAS: The Princess of the
South!

GONILLA *appears with her familiar, a monkey called* ENOCH, *on a tropical island. Her colours are green, flaming orange, gold and black.*

GONILLA (*sings*): My love breeds in the
tropical heat
Hanging upside down from palm trees
by its feet
My love's mango and my love's
peaches
And a million crawling and coiling
creatures
My love's an everglades alligator
And it hugs the world right round the
equator
And when my love beats
It goes bomp-a-bom-bomp
My love's doing
The stomp in the swamp

Rainforest fever and breadfruit pie
My love's brighter than the sun in your
eye
My love's simple as a bunch of bananas

Funky as a monkey that swings on
lianas
And if all that loving doesn't win me one
key
Daddy, you've made a monkey
out of me.
And when my love beats
It goes bomp-a-bom-bomp
My love's doing
The stomp in the swamp.

KING REAL: Gonilla, now your warm
tale is told,
Be Queen in the Power of the Key
of Gold

The ARCHBISHOP *hands over the gold key to* GONILLA. *She's transformed into a queen with crown and robes. Gold rain.* ALL *applaud.* KING REAL *and* GONILLA *embrace warmly.*

ARCHBISHOP: Has such mutual
affection, ever before,
been publicly demonstrated, and,
palpably, felt?

LORD THOMAS (*as answering a quiz question*): Yalta, '45 February 4 —
Churchill, Stalin and Roosevelt.

CLOUDELLA *has come on unnoticed, in a plain blue dress. She's followed by her woolly ginger dog,* RAINDOG.

CLOUDELLA: What shall Cloudella sing?
Love and be silent.

KING REAL (*seeing her and taking the crystal key from the* ARCHBISHOP):
Cloudella, Princess of the Sky,
Transparent as the Holy Crystal Key,
Youngest, favourite since you were so
high,
What can you sing of your love for me?

CLOUDELLA: Nothing, Father.

KING REAL: Nothing?

CLOUDELLA: Nothing.

KING REAL: Nothing will come of
nothing.
Sing to me.

CLOUDELLA: I can't sing today.
I love you as much as anyone could.

I think I love you as much as I should.
That's all.

KING REAL: That's all?

CLOUDELLA: You are my father.
I love you like your daughter.

KING REAL: You're young and tough.

CLOUDELLA: I'm young and truthful.

KING REAL: Don't you understand
what all this means?
The whole world's watching on their
TV screens.
An international Royal occasion,
The famous Good King Real's
abdication!
It's tribute time! According to plan,
His daughters pay compliments to the
old man.
Well, the first two do — with
pageantry, with song,
With eloquence — then comes along
Wearing a frown and an old blue sack
A sullen little duck too proud to
quack!
Don't give me nothing, Nothing — or
you'll be
Nothing yourself. Right — lose the
Crystal Key.

CLOUDELLA: I don't want keys and
power. I want nothing, father —

KING REAL: Nothing you'll get. Great
god, I'd rather
You'd not been born. Now, stand
aside.
Think of your future. Suicide?
Lord Thomas of Thomas, I know your
position
Is humble, a mere court musician,
But you have always been a friend to
me
So take, and guard, the Holy Crystal
Key.

LORD THOMAS: That's not my key.

ARCHBISHOP: What does that mean?

LORD THOMAS: Music, not politics,
that's my scene,
And, though I've been your friend, old
feller,
I'm even friendlier with Cloudella.

So you can take your holy key, old
chum,
And stick it where you stick your
chewing gum.

ARCHBISHOP: Lord Thomas of
Thomas! Have you lost your
reason?

RAYGAL: Obscenities!

GONILLA: Blasphemies!

RAYGAL: High Treason!

KING REAL: Wormwoody wangle-weed!
Wasp-warted wombat!
Now face the King's Champion in
single combat!

ARCHBISHOP: King's Champion! I
summon the King's Champion!

Suddenly CAPTAIN ADDERMAN,
*a very neat, tough, smooth army man
appears. Under his arm he carries, like
a swagger-stick, a metallic, extendable
tube.*

ADDERMAN: I'm at your service,
Captain Adderman.

ADDERMAN *bows to* KING REAL.
He kisses the hands of RAYGAL *and*
GONILLA. *He is motioned by* KING
REAL *not to approach* CLOUDELLA.

ARCHBISHOP: There stands the man
you must cut down to size.

ADDERMAN (*smiles*): Lord Thomas of
Thomas — what a surprise!
Thought you were too busy with your
tunes and stuff . . .
Never imagined that *you'd* cut up
rough.
However . . . not my business . . . well,
all right,
Let's get it over with —

LORD THOMAS: I don't fight.

ADDERMAN: Makes it much easier if
you don't
But hardly sporting.

KING REAL: Fight!

LORD THOMAS: I won't.

RAYGAL: Slaughter him.

GONILLA: Splatter him!

CLOUDELLA: Spare him.

LORD THOMAS: Yes!

ADDERMAN: Why don't I just give him a touch of BS?

LORD THOMAS: What's BS?

ADDERMAN: Don't worry, there isn't much pain.

LORD THOMAS: BS?

ADDERMAN: Brain Scrambler. It scrambles the brain.
Microwave spin-off. Plays a useful role —
Riot situations. Crowd control.

CLOUDELLA *tries to pull the BS tube away from him as he raises it. Infuriated,* KING REAL *comes forward and strikes at her with the crystal key, knocking her unconscious.* RAINDOG *guards her.* KING REAL *nods to* ADDERMAN. ADDERMAN *levels the tube at* LORD THOMAS *and carefully extends and adjusts the tube.*

ADDERMAN: There's the question of the adjustment Your Majesty. The lunacy level, we call it. Would you prefer delirium, idiocy, maniac or vegetable?

KING REAL: Raving idiocy.

ADDERMAN: Temporary or permanent, sire?

KING REAL: Permanent. Get it over with.

LORD THOMAS: I'll play one last tune. (*He begins to play his instrument.*)

RAYGAL: Let him have it.

GONILLA: Now.

ADDERMAN *fires. Terrible noise and light. The instrument screams,* LORD THOMAS *falls, holding his head. The treatment continues.*

KING REAL: That'll do.

ADDERMAN *stops firing at once.* GONILLA *and* RAYGAL *are*

disappointed. CLOUDELLA *is only just coming round.*

ARCHBISHOP: Pity it had to be carried that far,
But, as the Good Book says, *que sera sera.*
It's an imperfect seed that we spring from —

POOR TOM (*formerly* LORD THOMAS): Fathom and half, fathom and half; Poor Tom.

CLOUDELLA: Lord Thomas, here's my hand. Take hold.

POOR TOM: Bless your five senses — Tom's a-cold.

CLOUDELLA: I'm Cloudella, your friend. I'll never leave you.

POOR TOM: Poor Tom.

KING REAL: Everyone hear my Royal command.
If Cloudella is seen on Angalish land After tonight
She must be shot on sight.

RAYGAL: }
GONILLA: } That's right! That's right!

CLOUDELLA: Father, you'll not see me. What I said was true.
I'll give my love to those who need it more than you.

CLOUDELLA *leads* POOR TOM *away.* RAINDOG *goes with them.*

ARCHBISHOP: There remains the question of the Crystal Key.
Who shall the guardian of this treasure be?

KING REAL: Nobody could be more suitable than
My loyal Captain Adderman!

RAYGAL *and* GONILLA *applaud delightedly as* KING REAL *presents* ADDERMAN *with the crystal key.* ADDERMAN *is transformed into a general. Water rain. The three who have keys stand looking at each other, frozen in the realisation of their power.*

KING REAL (*stretches*): Retirement!
     Phew! It's good!

ARCHBISHOP: I've never tried it. How
     will you spend your time, sire?

KING REAL: I'll divide it
     Equally between my daughters. I've
          got two.
     Come, let's go think of something not
          to do.

KING REAL *and the* ARCHBISHOP
leave. RAYGAL, GONILLA *and*
GENERAL ADDERMAN *face each
other and begin to dance the dance of
the keys, as they sing. It's a bit like a
sword dance. Climax comes when all
three fit their keys together in a
triangle which is then held above the
head by each in turn, but ending with*
ADDERMAN.

RAYGAL (*sings*): The dance of the keys
     Is the dance of one
     The silver of swords
     And the silver gun

     And the dance of one
     Is a dance of stone
     And the dance of one
     Must be danced alone

     And the time of the dance
     It is zero hour
     And the dance of the keys
     Is the dance of power

GONILLA (*sings*): The dance of the keys
     Is the dance of two
     The rhythm of gold
     Swaying me and you

     And the dance of two
     Is a dance that tears
     And the dance of two
     Must be danced in pairs

     And the time of the dance
     It is zero hour
     And the dance of the keys
     Is the dance of power

ADDERMAN (*sings*): The dance of the
          keys
     Is the dance of three
     The music of pain
     And of destiny.

And the dance of three
As they skip and hop
Is the dance for three
That must never stop

And the time of the dance
It is zero hour
And the dance of the keys
Is the dance of power.

Scene Two

The road to the wasteland.
     *A yellow brick road, leading to a little
hill, spirally.* CLOUDELLA, TOM
(*formerly* LORD THOMAS OF
THOMAS) *and* RAINDOG *find the
beginning of the road. The sound of
hunting horns.*

CLOUDELLA: Adderman and my sisters
          hunt me down.
     So I'll transform myself into a clown.

CLOUDELLA, *with the help of*
RAINDOG, *transforms herself, with
make-up and costume, into a bright
clown. Meanwhile* POOR TOM
transforms himself into TOM
O'BEDLAM. *A long staff, an ox-horn
at his side, a sackcloth garment,
covered all over with ribbons, feathers,
cuttings of cloth, saucepans, dolls etc.
Iron ring on his left arm. A mad hat.*

TOM (*sings as they transform*): From the
          hag and hungry goblin
     That into rags would rend ye,
     All the spirits that stand
     By the naked man,
     In the book of moons defend ye.
     That of your five sound senses
     You never be forsaken;
     Nor travel from
     Yourselves with Tom
     Abroad to beg your bacon.

TOM
CLOUDELLA } (*sing*):
RAINDOG
     Nor never sing any food and feeding,
     Money, drink or clothing;

Come dame or maid,
Be not afraid,
For Tom will injure nothing.

TOM: Of thirty bare years have I
Twice twenty been enragéd;
And of forty been
Three times fifteen
In durance soundly cagéd.
In the lovely lofts of Bedlam,
In stubble soft and dainty,
Brave bracelets strong,
Sweet whips, ding, dong,
And a wholesome hunger plenty.

TOM
CLOUDELLA } (sing):
RAINDOG

Nor never sing any food and feeding,
Money, drink or clothing;
Come dame or maid,
Be not afraid,
For Tom will injure nothing.

CLOUDELLA: Come friends, let's climb
to the top of this mound
From up there the fox can watch out
for the hound.

The three begin to climb the hill.

TOM (*sings*): With a thought I took for
Maudlin,
And a cruse of cockle pottage,
And a thing thus — tall,
Sky bless you all,
I fell into the dotage.
I slept not till the Conquest;
Till then I never wakéd,
Till the roguish boy
Of love where I lay,
Me found and stripped me naked.

TOM
CLOUDELLA } (sing):
RAINDOG

Nor never sing any food and feeding,
Money, drink or clothing;
Come dame or maid,
Be not afraid,
For Tom will injure nothing.

They stand at the top of the hill. TOM
*is at the height of a painful vision and
the others know it.*

TOM (*declaims to music*): With a heart of
furious fancies,
Whereof I am commander:
With a burning spear
And a horse of air,
To the wilderness I wander;
With a knight of ghosts and shadows
I summoned am to Tourney;
Ten leagues beyond
The wide world's end;
Methinks it is no journey!

CLOUDELLA *and* RAINDOG
embrace TOM. *He collapses suddenly.*
CLOUDELLA *takes out a clown
telescope and scans the landscape. She
suddenly stops and jumps up.*

CLOUDELLA: My father! My sisters —
that poisonous pair!
Captain Adderman — now a general.
My Lord of Stare.
I see them on the stairway that leads
down
To the Royal Bunker, far
underground.
And now they are closing that great
iron door.
It is locked, like their hearts. They
prepare for war.
Come, Raindog. Come, Poor Tom —
(*She sings:*) With a heart of furious
fancies
Whereof I am commander:
With a burning spear
And a horse of air,
To the wilderness I wander;
With a knight of ghosts and shadows
I summoned am to Tourney:
Ten leagues beyond
The wide world's end;
Methinks it is no journey.

CLOUDELLA *leads* TOM *and*
RAINDOG *away, towards the
Wasteland.*

Scene Three

*The royal bunker.
An enclosed space, like a concrete*

womb, a bandshell. A tunnel leads away from it, upwards, towards the open air. It would be good to see this tunnel . . . Steps leading upwards surrounded by a tubular, semi-transparent, earth-coloured cloth. Lights along this tunnel. Big doors at the top. I would like to see RAYGAL, GONILLA, GENERAL ADDERMAN, ARCHBISHOP OF STARE, HOTPOINT *and* ENOCH *descending this stairway into the royal bunker. With them, in holiday mood,* KING REAL, *with a hip flask from which he swigs. Others are rather more earnest.*

They reach the bunker itself. The bunker has three desks with consoles, switches, buttons etc. At the moment the three desks are laid for dinner, so their true nature, as missile control desks, is not apparent. Tablecloths on the desks have the colours of the three key owners – RAYGAL – GONILLA – *and* ADDERMAN.

Apart from the desks and consoles, the bunker is a place of mirrors, mikes, lights, a considerable amount of property of all kinds which is to be preserved, including various works of art like Michaelangelo's David, the Mona Lisa etc. There is also a lot of food and drink. In fact the bunker should be a bit of an obstacle course and while, outside in the wasteland, people should seem tiny, in here people should seem huge. HOTPOINT *and* ENOCH *should be, until the launching, continually bringing more crates of stuff down from the big doors. Each crate, when opened, should contain a surprise.*

ARCHBISHOP: Now that we are safely gathered together in – er –

KING REAL: The royal bunker –

ARCHBISHOP: The royal bunker, I would like to recite the Collect for the King.

All bow their heads, except KING REAL, *who looks round the bunker cheerfully.*

Almighty God, whose Kingdom is everlasting and power infinite; have mercy upon the whole Church; and so rule the heart of thy chosen servant Real, our King and Governor, that he, (knowing whose minister he is) may above all things seek Thy honour and glory: and that we, and all his subjects (duly considering Whose authority he hath), may faithfully serve, honour and humbly obey him, in Thee, and for Thee, according to Thy Blessed word and ordinance; through Jesus Christ our Lord, Who, with Thee and the Holy Ghost liveth and reigneth, ever One God, world without end, Amen.

KING REAL: Thanks a lot. Very nice.

RAYGAL: General Adderman, are you sure we'll be safe here?

ADDERMAN: Safe as houses, your majesty.

RAYGAL: My sister and I are very safety-conscious, aren't we, Gonilla?

GONILLA: You bet your sweet belly-button.

RAYGAL *and* GONILLA *sing to* ADDERMAN, *seductively, while* HOTPOINT *and* ENOCH *lay sumptuous tables of food.*

RAYGAL
GONILLA } (*sing*):

Some girls are searching for marzipan visions
Some of them want nothing but eternal laughter
Some want a surgeon to make their decisions
But these girls know exactly what they are after –

RAYGAL (*sings*): I want a town that has no people
So I'm never in a crowd
I want a town that has no people
Where strangers aren't allowed
I want the countryside disinfected
So that stinging nettles won't grow
And a maximum security prison
For everyone I don't know.

RAYGAL ⎱
GONILLA ⎰ (*sing*):

Then I'll be safe
That's what I said
Safer than insurance
Safer than the dead
I want to be the safest person
In this dangerous dangerous world
Maximum security girl.

GONILLA (*sings*): I want a house that
has no windows
So the sun can't hurt my skin
I want a house that has no windows
So the neighbours can't look in
I want a maximum security garden
With land-mines planted in the ground
And a hundred and one alsatians
And electric fences all around.

RAYGAL ⎱
GONILLA ⎰ (*sing*):

Then I'll have peace
That's what I said
Safer than insurance
Safer than the dead
I want to be the safest person
In this dangerous dangerous world
Maximum security girl.

KING REAL: You know something.
Eating makes me thirsty. But drinking
makes me hungry. There's a funny
thing.

GONILLA: I think Queen Raygal has
prepared lunch for you.

RAYGAL: I believe we can manage one
extra for lunch. You'll be dining with
Gonilla tonight, I take it?

KING REAL (*putting robes on the back
of a chair, sitting down to eat with
GONILLA*): Well, I'm not sure yet.
Let you know later. What's cooking,
eh?

RAYGAL (*to the* PENGUIN): Bring the
King's lunch, Hotpoint.

HOTPOINT *with considerable
ceremony, brings a dish covered with a
silver salver. Leaving, he manages to
take* KING REAL's *robes off the back
of his chair and stash them.*

KING REAL: Aha! A dish fit for a — (*He
lifts the salver. There is a sardine tin
and a tin opener on a plate, plus one
leaf of lettuce.*) What? Ah, Raygal,
your sense of humour, wonderful joke,
wonderful.

RAYGAL: Eat your luncheon.

KING REAL: Don't frown. Joke over.
What? A tin of sardines and a lettuce
leaf. I've farted better meals.

RAYGAL: These are hard times.

KING REAL: I am the King.

RAYGAL: You were the King. (KING
REAL *swigs from his hipflask.*) And
give me that brandy.

RAYGAL *grabs the flask and empties
it on the ground.* KING REAL,
enraged, jumps to his feet.

KING REAL: Darkness and devils. Where
are my robes?

RAYGAL: Who knows?

KING REAL: Degenerate bastard, I'll not
trouble you. I've got another daughter.

RAYGAL: And she's welcome to you.

KING REAL *stomps over to where
GONILLA is scoffing, takes off his
jacket, puts it over the back of a chair,
sits down and looks at GONILLA's
plate.*

KING REAL: Looks good, what is it?

GONILLA: Roast breast of swan with
geranium sauce,
Pommes lyonnaises and candied yams,
Washed down with Mouton-Cadet 61.

KING REAL: Lovely. I'll have a large
one.

GONILLA: Surely it's Thursday.

KING REAL: Yes.

GONILLA: Today you lunch with
Raygal.

KING REAL: My darling Gonilla, listen
to me.
Your sister's nothing. She's cruel and
ungrateful.

You'd not believe how vile, O dear
Gonilla.

GONILLA: My sister? I can't believe it.
Have you been *drinking?* You know
she doesn't like you drunk.
Well, nobody does, but when you were
King
No one could stop you. But if you're
hungry,
I expect Enoch can rustle something
up.

ENOCH *arrives with golden plate and
a salver. He leaves, taking* KING
REAL's *jacket.*

KING REAL: Swan's always been my
favourite. Royal food. (*He lifts up the
salver.*) What's this? A packet of salted
peanuts.

GONILLA: These are hard times.

KING REAL: I was the King.

GONILLA: And now you're an old man
And cranky with it. Go back to
Raygal,
Tell her you're sorry, ask her to
forgive you.

KING (*getting down on his knees*): Like
this?
Dear daughter, I confess that I am old.
Age is embarrassing, I'm very sorry.
Please will you let me have some
clothes,
Some food and drink and a bed to
die in?

GONILLA: That's enough now. Go to
my sister.

KING: Never.

RAYGAL *comes over.*

RAYGAL: Poor Gonilla. Is he upsetting
you?

KING REAL: Don't talk to her, Gonilla.

GONILLA: Why not? You're getting
weird in your old age.

KING REAL: Please daughter, please,
don't make me mad.

RAYGAL: Wouldn't take much.

GONILLA: Just a slight scratch.

RAYGAL: It's not far from here
To the booby-hatch.

KING REAL (*rising up, beginning to
walk in his shirtsleeves, up the
staircase out of the bunker, sings*):

Rapped over simple reggae riffs

I'll get my own back on you both.
I'll do such things
I'll do such things
I don't know what they are
But I'll do such things
And they shall be
The terrors of the earth
The terrors of the earth.

You think I'll weep
You think I'll weep
I've got a lot to weep for
But I'll never weep.

I'll do such things
I'll do such things
I don't know what they are
But I'll do such things
And they shall be
The terrors of the earth
Terrors of the earth.

And my heart will break
Into a hundred thousand pieces
And each piece shall contain
The terrors of the earth.

And the earth will break
Into a hundred thousand pieces
And a hundred thousand terrors
But I'll never weep.

I'll weep such things
I'll weep such things
I don't know what they are
But I'll weep such things
And they shall be
The terrors of the earth
The terrors of the earth.

KING REAL *slams the bunker door.*
RAYGAL *and* GONILLA *are shaken.*
The ARCHBISHOP *comes to them.*
ADDERMAN *puts his arms round
both of them.*

ARCHBISHOP: You must remember —
he's a very old man.

ADDERMAN: You must *forget*. I'll help
you. You know that I can.

ADDERMAN, RAYGAL *and*
GONILLA *smile and embrace*.

ARCHBISHOP (*to* HOTPOINT *and*
ENOCH): You two — go shut the
doors!

Scene Four

The cold Wasteland
Very cold. CLOUDELLA, POOR TOM
and RAINDOG *walk through the*
Wasteland.

CLOUDELLA (*sings*): With my dear Tom
of Bedlam ten thousand years I'll
travel,
Cloudella goes with dirty shoes to save
her shoes from gravel.

CLOUDELLA: }
POOR TOM: }
Yet I will sing, bonny boys, bonny
mad boys, Bedlam boys are bonny,
They still go bare; and live by the air,
and want no drink nor money.

This is the chorus and is repeated
between every verse with as many as
will join in.

CLOUDELLA: I'm sorry now that my
poor Tom was ever so disdainéd,
My wits got lost when him I crossed
and that's why I go chainéd.

Chorus.

My staff has murdered giants, my bag
a long knife carries,
To cut mincepies from children's
thighs to feed unto the fairies.

Chorus.

My horn is made of thunder, I stole it
out of heaven,
The rainbow there is this I wear, for
which I thence was driven.

Chorus.

I went to Pluto's kitchen, to beg some
food one morning,
And there I got souls, piping hot, with
which the spits were turning.

Chorus.

Then I took up a cauldron, where
boiled ten thousand harlots,
Twas full of flame, yet I drank the
same, to the health of all such
varlets.

Chorus.

A spirit, hot as lightning, did in that
journey guide me,
The sun did shake, and the pale moon
quake, as soon as e'er they spied
me.

Chorus.

And now that I have gotten a lease,
then doomsday's no longer,
To live on earth, with some in mirth,
ten whales shall feed my hunger.

Chorus.

No gypsy-slut or doxy shall win my
mad Tom from me,
We'll weep all night, and with stars
fight, the fray will well become me.

Chorus.

And when that I have beaten the man
in the moon to powder,
His dog I'll take and him I'll make as
could no daemon longer.

Chorus.

A health to Tom-A-Bedlam, go fill the
sea in barrels,
I'll drink it all, well brewed with gall,
and maudling drinks I'll quarrel.

ALL: Yet I will sing, bonny boys, bonny
mad boys, Bedlam boys are bonny
They still go bare, and live by the air,
and want no drink or money.

KING REAL *comes on, staggering. His*
shirt is dirty and torn, he has been
walking a long way. CLOUDELLA
sees him coming, recognises him, hides
behind POOR TOM.

KING REAL: Who's there?

TOM: Poor Tom's a-cold.

KING REAL: Did your daughters bring you to this?

CLOUDELLA (*disguising voice*): He has no daughters, sir.

KING REAL: Who's that?

CLOUDELLA: A mouldy clown without a circus.

TOM: Tom's a-cold.

CLOUDELLA: Well, we're all-a-bloody cold. We'd better find somewhere to sleep. This freezer of a night'll send us all crazy.

TOM: The Prince of Darkness is a gentleman.

KING REAL: I was more than a gentleman. I was —

CLOUDELLA: You were a man. You were a boy. You were a baby. You were many things you'll never be again.

KING REAL: I went to dinner with my daughters and they served me crap.

TOM: Poor Tom eats the swimming frog, the toad, the tadpole, the wall-newt, and the water. In the fury of his heart, when the foul Fiend rages, he eats cow-dung, swallows the old rat, and the ditch dog, drinks the green mantle of the standing pool.

Sings, from 'From the Hag and Hungry Goblin'.

I know more than Apollo
For oft, when he lies sleeping,
I behold the stars
At mortal wars,
And the rounded welkin weeping.
The moon embraces her shepherd,
And the Queen of Love her warriors;
While the first does horn
The stars of the morn,
And the next the heavenly farrier.

KING REAL: That's true, clown. No. Don't laugh at me. But this is Raindog. (RAINDOG *barks.*) And, as I'm a man this clown must be my child — Cloudella.

CLOUDELLA: And so I am. I am.

KING REAL *and* CLOUDELLA *both hold back.*

KING REAL: I hope you're sorry now.

CLOUDELLA: Not half as sorry as you.

KING REAL: Why did you shame me in front of the world?
I knew all along that you loved me best.

CLOUDELLA: You knew nothing. Listen. (*She sings, not dirge-like.*)

O no, I never loved you best of all
O no, I could not love you properly
For you controlled the ways
In which I spent my days
And you could order me to laugh or cry
And you could order me to live or die
Because I was your royal property
Because I was your royal property.

You were Father Christmas
And I longed for you
You were the hangman
And I hid from you
You were the ice-cream man
I worshipped you
You were the scissorman
I dreamed of you
How could I love you
When I always knew
I was the unicorn
In your concrete zoo?

And so I never loved you best of all
O no, I could not love you properly
Because you would not let me love you properly.

KING REAL: The world has gone mad and cold and thin.
I'll go back to my daughters. They will take me in.

KING REAL *runs away wildly.*
CLOUDELLA *stares after him.*
RAINDOG *howls.*

Scene Five

The royal bunker.
RAYGAL, GONILLA and
ADDERMAN at their desks. Their desks
have been stripped down — food and
tablecloths have gone.
The three look very business-like.
They wear earphones, have microphones,
watch consoles, mouth orders. Between
them run ENOCH and HOTPOINT with
papers, messages etc.
The ARCHBISHOP is broadcasting to
the nation.

ARCHBISHOP: So, finally, I would like
to remind you that the authorities
have asked you to bear three things in
mind, just in case the current world
crisis leads to an Emergency and the
Emergency leads to a Nuclear
Misunderstanding.
1. Do not go out of doors.
2. Place deceased persons and pets in
    black plastic bags and seal the bags.
3. After forty days and forty nights, it
    will be possible to leave your
    shelter.
Now may the peace of God which
passes all understanding be with you
now and always, keep smiling and —
have a good night.

The ARCHBISHOP switches himself
off. Sudden great battering at the
door.

ADDERMAN: See who it is, Archy.

ARCHBISHOP: All right.

The ARCHBISHOP trudges up the
stairs, opens the door a little, KING
REAL pushes in and past him.

KING REAL (*coming down the stairs*):
I'm back, girls, I'm back for good this
time.

RAYGAL (*to GONILLA*): Oh, he's back.

GONILLA: Back for good.

ADDERMAN: Nice.

KING REAL: Yes, I'm very sorry. I've
really been rather a foolish old man.

ADDERMAN: Foolish? Make it stupid.

KING REAL (*laughs*): Always did have a
sense of humour, Adderman.

ADDERMAN (*getting up*): Look, this is
the royal bunker, you know, a nuclear
shelter plus a missile command site
and we can't have psychotic geriatrics
popping in and out like it was the
Darby and Joan Club can we?

KING REAL: I suppose not but —

ADDERMAN: Please don't interrupt me
squire because I have what they call a
rather short fuse so I'm just asking you
in the nicest possible way to fuck off
out of here. Pronto.

RAYGAL: Get going.

GONILLA: On your bike.

KING REAL: Well, I'm not going.

ADDERMAN: Oh, you're not going?

RAYGAL: Throw him out.

GONILLA: On his royal arse.

ADDERMAN: Hang about. If we chuck
him out he'll just collect a gang and
come back and knock down the doors,
won't he? Unless . . .

RAYGAL: }
GONILLA: } Unless?

ADDERMAN: Archbishop, come here . . .
(*He whispers. The ARCHBISHOP nods*
and nods.) Hotpoint! Enoch! Tie him
to a chair.

HOTPOINT and ENOCH force KING
REAL into a chair and tie him with
wire, arms to arms of chair, legs apart.
ADDERMAN still briefing the
ARCHBISHOP. Music begins.
ARCHBISHOP assisted by GONILLA
and RAYGAL, begins to divest himself
of vestments. When he's down to his
long underpants, he begins to put on a
gown, then a little hat, mask and
finally gloves. He has become a
surgeon.

ARCHBISHOP (*to KING REAL*): It's
quite all right, I was a surgeon before
I entered the Church, and one never
forgets. It won't take two moments,

just a little prick here (*The bridge of his nose.*) and here (*Thigh.*) local anaesthetic wonderful how these things have developed and scoop please (GONILLA *as a nurse holds out a spoon-like instrument, he takes it and removes one of the* KING's *eyes with it.*) Eye tray please (RAYGAL *extends a tray, eye plops in.*) Scoop again, thank you (*Second eye out and into the tray.*) Tray. Good. Socket spray. (*Handed aerosol, sprays sockets.*) Lovely. Lovely.

All this time the KING *has been screaming silently, with an open mouth.*

GONILLA: Do you want the castrator now?

ARCHBISHOP: Yes, please m'dear.

But suddenly lights begin to flash and sirens to wail.

ADDERMAN: What is happening? Red alert. Get to your desks.

RAYGAL: What about the old man?

ADDERMAN: Hotpoint! Enoch! Throw him out.

HOTPOINT *and* ENOCH *unbind* KING REAL, *zoom him up the steps, out the door and lock the door after him.*

ADDERMAN, RAYGAL *and* GONILLA *get back to their desks. The* ARCHBISHOP *changes back into ecclesiastical garb.*

ADDERMAN, RAYGAL *and* GONILLA *produce their three keys from under their desks. They fit them into the top of the desks.*

Watch it. The missiles will only go off if we all turn our keys at the same moment.

ARCHBISHOP: Good luck.

ADDERMAN: Count it down with me.

ADDERMAN: } Ten, nine, eight, seven,
RAYGAL: } six, five, four, three,
GONILLA: } two, one, zero.

They turn their keys. All hell breaks loose.

Scene Six

The hot wasteland.

Firestorm. In the midst of the terrible storm, CLOUDELLA *and* POOR TOM *cling together.* RAINDOG *lies dead. They are howling their song against the storm.*

CLOUDELLA } (*sing from 'From the*
POOR TOM } *Hag and Hungry*
              Goblin'):
With a heart of furious fancies
Whereof I am commander:
With a burning spear
And a horse of air
To the wilderness I wander . . .

POOR TOM *stops singing.*

With a knight of ghosts and shadows
I am summoned to Tourney:
Ten leagues beyond
The wide world's end;
Methinks it is no journey.

CLOUDELLA: Lord Thomas.

He is dead. She lays him down. She begins to shake and hold on to herself with both arms. Nearer the audience, KING REAL, *blinded, makes his way on. He speaks to the audience.*

KING REAL: I crawled from the bunker towards the river. I found the iron railway bridge, but the metal rails were red hot. The crowds were screaming, and it sounded like one enormous voice.

I stumbled over some bodies which were still moving. Their skin was hanging from them like strands of seaweed. There were holes where their noses should be.

I could hear the roaring of the flames. I heard a woman call for her husband. I tried to take her arm, but her arm was on fire. I was crawling over the corpses, pushing them aside. I pulled the head of a corpse so that I could get by and the skin of its face stuck to my palms.

I clambered over a pile of corpses. I had to get over them. I could hear the cracking of their bones. At last the mountain of dead lay behind me. And then I heard her voice.

CLOUDELLA: Father, help me. Help me.

KING REAL *crawls towards her.*

KING REAL: Cloudella. Keep calling out. I'll find you.

CLOUDELLA: Father. Father. Father. Father.

KING REAL *reaches her. He takes her in his arms.*

KING REAL: Don't be frightened. My eyes don't hurt.

CLOUDELLA: Your eyes? I can't see.

KING REAL: Cloudella. I wish I could have loved you properly.

CLOUDELLA: Me too. You should have destroyed the keys, you know.

KING REAL: I know. Well, shall we die together?

CLOUDELLA: I'm sorry, Father, I can't wait. I'm sorry. It hurts! It hurts!

She dies.
    KING REAL *puts his hand to her heart and leans to her.*

KING REAL: Cloudella, stay a little. Ha: What are you saying? Her voice was always soft,
Gentle and low, an excellent thing . . .

KING REAL *picks her up in his arms.*

Howl, howl, howl: O you are men of stones
Had I your tongues and eyes, I'd use them so
That Heaven's vault should crack. She's gone forever.
I know when one is dead, and when one lives.
You'll come no more,
Never, never, never, never, never.

KING REAL *lies down with her in his arms. He dies.*

Scene Seven

The royal bunker.
    In the corner a large cauldron is seething. RAYGAL, GONILLA *and* ADDERMAN *watch as a strange game is enacted.*
    The ARCHBISHOP *holds a great globe on a pole. The cities are marked by bunches of embedded fireworks, unlit at first.* HOTPOINT *and* ENOCH *take turns to light them. Music. The* ARCHBISHOP *announces the name of each city as it is lit. All drink to the cities — all booze throughout this scene.*

ARCHBISHOP: Bonn.
            Sofia.
            Manchester.
            Warsaw.
            Milan.
            Prague.
            Paris.
            Bucharest.
            Jerusalem.
            Tripoli.
            London.
            Durban.
            Leningrad.
            Los Angeles.
            Pekin.
            Mexico City.
            Tokyo.
            Calcutta.
            Edinburgh.
            Kiev.
            Sydney.
            New York.

And now the globe itself is burning and they watch and watch until it burns out.

ADDERMAN (*applauds*): How long till it's safe for us to go out, Your Grace?

ARCHBISHOP (*consulting his wrist Geiger-counter*): Forty days and forty nights — give or take a day.

ADDERMAN: We'd better think up some party games to play.

ARCHBISHOP: How about something like Twenty Questions?

ADDERMAN: Come on. Let's have some grown-up suggestions.

RAYGAL (sings): Hunt the Blister
Who Gets the Goose?
Banana Dancing
Musical Noose
Or — imitate your favourite river.

GONILLA (sings): Pass the Finger
Juggling with rats
Tricks with crutches
Sterilising bats
Or — imitate your favourite window.

ADDERMAN (sings): Sur le pont
D'Avignon
Water's boiling water's boiling

ARCHBISHOP (sings): Treacle swinging
Suck the Rag
Who's In the Big Black
Polythene Bag?
Or — imitate your favourite currency.

ALL (sing chorus): May sound funny
But these are the names
Of some of the brave new
Party games.

RAYGAL (sings): Lemon swapping
Ripping Rippings
Build a cathedral
From your Toenail Clippings
Or — imitate your favourite plague.

GONILLA (sings): Ant Embalming
Rape the Clown
Agatha Christie's
Upside Down
Or — imitate your favourite
archipelago.

ALL (sing chorus): May sound funny
But these are the names
Of some of the brave new
Party games.

ADDERMAN (sings): Parents and
children have I none
But I have a shelter and I have a gun.

ARCHBISHOP: Ukelele races.

RAYGAL: Betting on Dreams.

GONILLA: Spit At The Mirror.

ADDERMAN: Come Apart At the Seams.

ALL (sing): There's plenty of others we
haven't played yet
Like How Many Dead People Can You
Forget?
And it
May sound funny
But these are the names
Of some of our brave new
Party games.

HOTPOINT *and* ENOCH *are moaning and rubbing their stomachs with hunger. The others exchange glances.*

RAYGAL: Games make me hungry, how about you?

GONILLA: I could eat a horse or a spider or a shrew.

ARCHBISHOP: I'm feeling a bit peckish too.

ADDERMAN: Well, howsabout Penguin and Monkey Stew?

This is a cue for all four of them to leap upon the hapless penguin and monkey and push them in the seething cauldron. RAYGAL and GONILLA stir the cauldron.

ARCHBISHOP: Forty days and nights go fast when you're having fun.

ADDERMAN: Time to go out and rekky.

RAYGAL: No.

GONILLA: Not you.

ARCHBISHOP: You're needed at the instruments.

ADDERMAN: Then who?

RAYGAL: I think I'm pregnant.

GONILLA: I may well be.

ADDERMAN: Yes, it's a problem.

ARCHBISHOP: That leaves me. I'm glad to go. And I may find, perhaps, Some life still left up there. Wish me luck, chaps.

The ARCHBISHOP climbs up the stairs to portentous music. He stops at the door, looks round. The others urge him to go on, then they take another drink. The ARCHBISHOP opens the door a little way. A shaft of light hits him. He is frozen for a moment, then manages to close the door and turn.

Half his face and the side of his robes are streaked with black zigzags. He has been stricken by radioactivity.

Will someone take my money? It's burning me. There's a rat! Stamp its skull out. Peace.

The rockets stood up in the air. Then they screamed away like foaming giants.

Staggering down steps.

RAYGAL (*eating stew*): Is the door properly shut?

ARCHBISHOP: Tight as the Pearly Gates.

GONILLA (*eating stew*): If you're coming back down here, what's the password?

ARCHBISHOP: Bitter flesh.

ADDERMAN (*eating stew*): Pass, friend.

ARCHBISHOP: Are you the King?

ADDERMAN: Sure. I'm the King.

ARCHBISHOP: If you're the King, you should kill all these monsters. They burn, they scald, they stink, they devour. Morphia, morphia! We are all monsters, so let's forgive each other.

RAYGAL (*to* ADDERMAN): Don't go near him. He's radioactive.

ARCHBISHOP: I'm on the wheel of fire. I'm choking. Please, please, please, please — undo this button.

GONILLA (*with Geiger-counter*): He's driving the Geiger-counter crazy. What do we do?

ADDERMAN: Fetch one of the bags. Get it over his head.

RAYGAL and GONILLA come up behind the ARCHBISHOP with a large, strong, black plastic bag.

ARCHBISHOP. Undo this button.

RAYGAL and GONILLA pull the bag over his head, upturn him, stuff him in. ADDERMAN ties up the top of the bag. The ARCHBISHOP continues to wriggle for some time.

RAYGAL: There's only one snag I can see.

Who'll marry the General to me?

GONILLA: Sorry, sister step aside. He booked me to be his bride.

RAYGAL: You venereal sewer-rat!

GONILLA: Right. There's only one answer to that.

GONILLA slaps RAYGAL, who steps back.

RAYGAL: You give me trouble, I'll give you double.

RAYGAL punches GONILLA hard. GONILLA recovers.

GONILLA: My girl, you're going to end up rubble.

GONILLA gets RAYGAL in a wrestling hold, throws her over her shoulder, jumps on her. The fight develops. RAYGAL lets GONILLA have it with a boot. GONILLA pulls darts from a dartboard and showers RAYGAL with them. Luckily they miss. RAYGAL pulls a knife from her boot and goes for GONILLA. GONILLA kicks it away, manages to grab a long truncheon with a flail (see Bruce Lee). RAYGAL counters with a javelin, advances on GONILLA prodding her up against the wall.

You can have him. No! (*As RAYGAL prods.*) But think of the future. Maybe you won't be able to have kids. Then he'll have to screw me. Just for the future.

RAYGAL: Bit late to think about the future, honey.

RAYGAL kills her with the javelin. GONILLA collapses. RAYGAL turns and walks, triumphant, towards ADDERMAN. ADDERMAN smiles, produces a revolver, shoots RAYGAL three times. She collapses beside her sister.

*This is a rhythmic rap, accompanied
possibly by percussion. A good
interpretation is included on Welfare
State's* King Real *tape.*

ADDERMAN (*sings*): My mother was a
    desert
My father was a bone
And I was born
To burn the world to stone.

I went to school at Nightmare
They taught me how to fear
I want to slit the human race
From ear to ugly ear.

Cos I'm crazy 'bout nothing
Gotta have that good nothing
Gimme my sweet nothing
Nothing nothing.

Working in a factory
Smoke and slamming steel
Sucking on the valium
Until I couldn't feel.

Found myself redundant
Buggered off to rot
Came back pleading for a job
Nothing's what I got.

Now I'm crazy 'bout nothing
Gotta have that good nothing
Gimme sweet nothing
Nothing nothing.

Joined the British Army
Learned a steady trade
British Army showed me
How nothing is made

And now

Nothing is my woman
We live in Nothing Town
On a nothing planet
That we just burned down.

Cos we're crazy 'bout nothing
Gotta have that good nothing
Gimme my sweet nothing
Nothing nothing.

ADDERMAN *climbs to the top of the
stairs.*

Should be safe now.

ADDERMAN *opens the door. A great
light.* ADDERMAN *freezes. A scarlet
flood – represented by rolling cloth,
topples him down the stairs to join the
other corpses, engulfing them all.
Stillness. Silence. A bird sings. The
bird stops singing. Silence.*
    LORD THOMAS THE THOMAS
enters as in Scene One, in single spot.

LORD THOMAS: I saw a vision on my
    vision machine
I saw a vision but what did it mean?
They burned the sea and they burned
    the air
And I was drowning in my own
    despair
Till I tore that vision from the vision
    machine
And I played a different vision that I
    never had seen
Pretty as a vision you know what I
    mean?

LORD THOMAS *indicates* KING
REAL *and* CLOUDELLA. KING
REAL *is on the throne as in Scene
One.* CLOUDELLA *with* RAINDOG
as in Scene One. Each in a spot light.

KING REAL: Cloudella, Princess of the
    Sky,
Transparent as the Holy Crystal Key,
Youngest, favourite since you were so
    high,
What can you sing of your love for
    me?

CLOUDELLA: Nothing, Father.

KING REAL: Nothing?

CLOUDELLA: Nothing.

KING REAL: Nothing will come of
    nothing.
Sing to me.

CLOUDELLA: I can't sing today.
I love you as much as anyone could.
I think I love you as much as I should.
That's all.

KING REAL: That's all?

CLOUDELLA: You are my father.
I love you like your daughter.

KING REAL: I can see the deep blue love
in your eyes.
Your love walks naked with no
disguise
It shames me as it shames your sisters'
lies.
I love you Cloudella, but what can I
do?

CLOUDELLA: Do you love this planet?

KING REAL: Yes, I love this planet.

CLOUDELLA: Those keys will destroy
it.

KING REAL: No. I'll destroy the keys.

CLOUDELLA: I love you.

As they destroy the keys, LORD
THOMAS *walks forward and sings:*

LORD THOMAS (*sings*): When man first
flew beyond the sky
He looked back into the world's blue
eye
Man said: what makes your eye so
blue?
Earth said: the tears in the oceans do.
Why are the seas so full of tears?
Because I've wept so many thousand
years.
Why do you weep as you dance
through space?
Because I am the mother of the human
race.

THE TRAGEDY OF KING REAL

Music for the Play

KING REAL

This is performed as a processional chant involving 2 groups of chorus and a number of solos. Accompanied preferably by strong percussion.

1: King Real
   King Real
   King Real
   King Real
   King Real
   King Real

2: Rules the land and the sea
   To the power of three
   All victorious
   Ultra glorious
   Real as real estate
   Real as the wheel of fate

SOLO 1: You'd better get your knees in training to kneel

2: Practice crawling on your belly like an eel

3: He'll run you over in his royalmobile

ALL   King Real   that Real King   King Real

(rules the land and . . .)

Chorus repeats.

Other verses treated similarly.

Speech rhythms dictate the chant.

Po-lar bear's white fu-ry as he kills——— ter-ror of the hunter as his

ka-yak o-ver-turns——— Endless-ness of land-scapes of white de-serts and white hills———

mon-strous him-a-la-yas where the yet-ti——— yearns——— That's how I love you———

Wild as a bliz-zard——— That's how I love you——— Big as a bliz-zard———

That's how I love you——— Blind Blind Blind as a Bliz-zard———

(See arrangement.)

2nd verse to same melody shape.

STOMP IN THE SWAMP

SLEAZY

E7♭II   A7

carries through
first section

MELODY SHOULD BE FREE AND BLUESY

E7♭II   A7   etc.

My love breeds in the tro-pi-cal heat   Hang-ing up-side-down from the

palm trees by its feet   My love's man-go   My love's pea-ches and a

mil-lion coi-ling   craw-ling crea-tures My love's an e-ver-glades-al-li-

ga-tor   And it hugs the worldright round the e— qua-tor   And when my

love beats   it goes Boppe-di-bomp ——   My love's do-ing   the

Stompin the swamp And when my love beats   it goes Bomp-pe-di-bomp—

My love's do-ing   the   Stompin the swamp ——

dmin   emin

F   emin   dmin   emin   F   emin

Rain for-est fe-ver —— bread-fruit pie—

etc.

My love's brighter than the sun in your eye—— My love's sweeter than a

bunch of ba-na-nas   Fun-ny as a mon-key that swings on li-a-nas If

all that lov-ing does-n't win me one key   Dad-dy . . . . .

you've made a mon-key out of me.   And when my love beats etc . . . .

VICIOUS

Dance of the keys

Dance of one silver of swords silver gun the Dance of one is the dance of stone

Dance of one must be danced a-lone the Time Time of the dance it is

ze-ro hour Dance of the keys is the Dance of

Pow-er

unaccompanied, freely

From the hag and hun—gry go-blin   that in-to

Of   your five sand sen-ses etc.

rags would rend ye   All   the spi-rits that stand by the na-ked man

In the book of moons de-fend ye   That Name-ver

sing a-ny food and fee-ding   Mon-ey drink or

clo-thing   Come dame or maid Be not a-fraid   For

Tom will en-dure no-thing

Rhythm feel is 3/4 vs. 6/8.
See 3rd to last bar and extend
throughout song.

I ne-ver loved you best of all   Oh no I ne-ver loved you pro-per-ly

You con-trolled the ways in which I spent my days   You could or-der me to

laugh or cry   You could or-der me to live or die   Because I was your Royal property.

MORE RHYTHMIC

You were fa-ther Christmas and I longed for you, you were the hang man   I

hid from you   The   ice cream man I   wor-shipped you   the

scissor man   I   dreamed   of   you   How could I love you when I

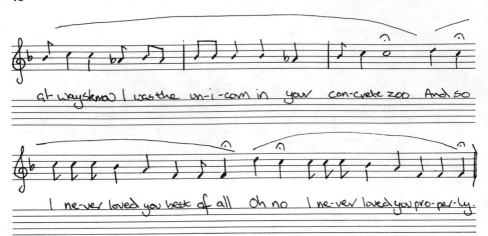

at waysk말 I was the un-i-corn in your con-crete zoo And so

I ne-ver loved you best of all Oh no I ne-ver loved you pro-per-ly.

MANIC

(parlando)

Hunt the Bli – ster who gets the goose Ba – na – na danc–ing

Musi–cal noose or imitate . . . . imitate . . . .

"imitate" "imitate"

imitate _ your favourite river   Sur le pont D'Avig–non

wa–tersboiling wa–tersboiling May sound funny but these are the games of

some of our brave new party   games

SLOW ♩ = 60

when man first flew be-yond the sky when man first flew be-yond the

sky   he   looked back into the world's blue eyes he looked back into the world's blue eyes be-

yond the sky   the   world's blue eye   Mother of our   race

Underlying rhythm (osi drum, muffled xylophone etc.)

1 2 3   4   1 2   3   1   2 3   1 2

THE CELEBRATION OF KOKURA

**A play to be performed by young people,
using music, dance and improvisation**

Berta Freistadt is a poet and playwright. Her work for the theatre includes *Keeley's Mother* (Theatre Royal, London E15 Studio Theatre, 1981), which was a prize-winner in the Capital/GLAA Play Awards of 1981; *Poor, Silly, Bad* (Theatre Venture, 1982); *The Burning Time* (Theatre Venture, 1983); and *A Fine Undertaking* (Oval House, 1984). She is also an actress, a short story writer, and gives readings of her own poetry.

The Celebration of Kokura

In 1968 I took up my first teaching post in the East End of London. A nicely brought up, sensitive young woman, I was eager to serve and so had reservations about the girls' high school I had been appointed to. In my experience 'high school' meant nice manners, tea on the lawn and corridors of whispering damsels. I needn't have worried. My first term there was such a revelation to me that I wonder now why I didn't go into shock. It was by reputation the hardest school in the borough. Stories were rife, though myth usually paled in the face of reality. Indeed it was not unusual for girls who attended to pretend that they went to a different school. Details I refuse to give — not to protect the innocent — but out of respect for those young women who gave us all such a hard time; a lot of them already by the age of eleven had knowledge of life that I'm still learning. Anyway, the moment I stepped in there I suffered instant loss of innocence, and no bad thing either. It was a crash course in survival and personal development. I stayed in the borough, though not with that school, for eight years, so I did at least survive.

I was a teenager in the fifties, and going on Aldermaston marches, at least part of the way, was practically obligatory. We were all aware, almost proud, of our identity that came with early consciousness of what living with The Bomb meant. Still, in 1970 it was by chance that a small report in the *Guardian* caught my eye. It told how the people of the Japanese town of Kokura gather every year to celebrate their escape one cloudy day, when an American pilot, unable to get a sight on their town, passed over them and dropped his load on the next on his list; Nagasaki.

I'd been looking for a subject for an end of term play and this immediately caught my imagination. I had been forced to write my own the previous year since there was nothing in print at all suitable for the youngsters I was working with. Nothing approached their experience, their energy, their culture or their language, let alone their sense of what was right or wrong, their sense of rebellion and drama. As I touted for a cast I also began to read. After all I knew nothing of the subject. Soon I was deep in Japanese culture, American guilt, the science of nuclear physics, and the history of the war. John Hershey's *Hiroshima* was the most important book I came across; an eye witness account with verbatim report. A lot of the play is John Hershey. I didn't ask his permission then, so I thank him now.

It was obvious to me that a realistic play was out of the question. 'My girls' didn't have the training for that. I knew I wanted to write something that was safe for them to perform. Thus I developed the idea of a narrator telling a story. The end result is very simple — there are three stories: the development of the bomb, the history of the war, and the personal accounts of a group of women. These are in easily rehearsable sections, punctuated by the comments of the two narrators. No youngster has too much to learn and everyone has her part.

At a dress rehearsal a member of the staff remarked rather scathingly that she thought on the whole they were rather drilled. Indeed that was my very aim; to drill these uncontrollable and explosive young women into performing on their own. I wanted none of the anxious teacher running around frantically at the last moment. I'd got the most reliable girl in the school, a fifth former, in charge of the sound system, another on the lights and there were the two narrators equipped and indeed drilled to punctuate and control the show. By the first performance they knew they were on their own, it was a bit like being in charge of a group of soldiers about to jump out of an aeroplane. That first entry procession, so silent, so dignified, took the audience, the parents, the staff and even the Head herself by surprise. It was a success that rocked the borough. Not that the play is such a great one, rather that these girls had achieved so much in public; for a few days the whole school was bathed in reflected glory.

If I've made a lot of all this, that school was my baptism of fire, I remember everything.

Berta Freistadt
November 1984

The Celebration of Kokura was first performed on 16 July 1970, at the Deanery High School for Girls, East London, with the following cast:

NARRATORS	Susan Booth
	Susan Poole
JAPAN	Karen Roach
UNITED STATES OF AMERICA	Judy Sellers
AMERICAN PRESIDENT	Maxine Griffin
MRS PEGGY CHURCH	Tina Glander
SCIENTISTS	Colleen Gray
	Janet Sawkins
MRS NAKAMURA	Lesley Groutage
MRS TANIMOTO	Harparkash Kaur
MRS KAMAI	Angela Gill
MRS MURATA	Susan Edwards
MISS SASAKI	Sharon Frazer
MRS SUZUKI	Angela West
YAEKO	Diane Scott
THE KATAOKA CHILDREN	Lesley Adams, Jacqueline Blasby, Tina Presland
DEATH	Joan Dear

Stage management: Marise Corbett, Pauline Douglas, Yvonne Haywood, Yvonne Hunter, Susan James, Deborah Seares, Janet Sergent, Brenda Webb
Photographers: Barbara Brown, Christine Saunderson

Enter a group of people — celebrating: joyous, yet solemn. Freeze. One breaks away, to the audience.

NARRATOR: We are celebrating. Every year it is the same. We climb up here and look down and are thankful. And we look up. This is no ancient paganism. This is not a celebration from a dead age. Although in a way it is. No! This ceremony is dead — sincerity springs from our hearts once a year on this spot. For the rest of the year we forget it.

They continue to move. They go.

We are in Japan — in a town called Kokura. Every year we climb to the top of this hill. In 1945 an aeroplane passed over our city because it was covered with cloud. The plane carried a deadly atom bomb. It was scheduled to be dropped on us, but as the pilot's sights found only cloud he flew to another city and dropped his load there.

Every year we celebrate.

MRS NAKAMURA: May I present myself to you. I am Hatsuyo Nakamura and these are Toshio, Yaeko and Myeko. We live in the Nobovicho area. Isawa, my husband, was a tailor, but five years ago he left us to go with the army. Since then I heard nothing from him, until I got this telegram — 'Isawa died an honourable death at Singare.' He left us no money — so I took his sewing machine and started to do piece work. It supports us. At midnight before the bomb came we were all told over the radio to go to the East Parade Ground air raid shelter. So I dressed the children and we went. By the time we'd got there and unrolled our sleeping mats and slept a little it was two o'clock. The sound of planes woke us. Then we went home and when I switched on the radio there was another air raid warning — but the children were so tired, we couldn't go again. I decided to risk it and we all went to sleep. At seven the siren started and didn't stop till eight. I was looking out of the window when suddenly:

Chorus.

In the land of the Rising Sun
A new sun has risen
A sun of destruction
Of agony and death.

Verse One
Old paintings have shown
Quiet waters and a still wind
Or the silent smiles of lovers
Since this new invention
Our pictures are red
Red with the blood
Of fingerless artists.

Verse Two
Our music was played
To enliven hearts
To sooth the spirit
Or to imitate birdsong
Today instruments echo
Screams of the dying
And the noise of fire.

Verse Three
Long ago poets wrote
Of love in rhyme and metre
Of brave deeds
And clever words
Of Emperors and Kings
Today our tales
Are tales of death.

Verse Four
Yesterday war was
The concern of the Samurai
The professional soldiers
Nowadays it is
The housewives who die
Nowadays we see
The blood of fishmongers.

NARRATOR: At the start of the Second World War, Japan had been busy expanding her territory in the Pacific. She had built up her navy and had occupied Pacific islands. When Germany defeated Holland and France, Japan hoped to take over their Pacific colonies. Only Britain and America offered any opposition and in

1941 Japan occupied Indo-China. America tried to persuade Japan to move out of Indo-China and make a settlement, but she refused. This refusal was strengthened by a new general. Hideki Tojo — nicknamed 'the razor'.

In December 1941 America's Pacific Fleet in a place called Pearl Harbour was put out of action by a Japanese surprise attack. After this Japan captured more and more territory. But between 1943 and 1944 she lost it and began to suffer heavily in battle. Some people say that Japan was ready to surrender — but others claim that Japan would fight to the last soldier.

UNITED STATES: Yet by number alone it would have cost America millions of men to have defeated Japan. She had her Kamikaze pilots who flew to their death by aiming their bomb-filled aircraft at our ships. We could only destroy them by bombing. They had many more men than we did.

JAPAN: But the Americans made a blockade. We could get no raw materials for armaments or fuel. Nor could the fishing fleets go out. They had made so many homeless with their bombing — there were no thick clothes nor fuel for the winter. No food. A whole family would live on one person's ration. People used to go into the country on Sundays to dig roots and pick berries.

BOY: I remember standing in the sun under the temple caves, sniffing tooth powder to forget my hunger.

NARRATOR: By 1945 they were starving and exhausted. Terrified by air raids; hating their own soldiers and frightened by their military police who arrested anyone who whispered the word 'surrender'. The country was quite war weary. Rumour said the Emperor wanted surrender but that the army was too strong for him. Anyway the Americans' condition of surrender said 'unconditional surrender'. And the Japanese could not accept these words.

JAPAN: We have been taught to adore our Emperor as you Europeans do your god. Therefore to surrender was not possible. The idea of allowing foreigners to dictate to our Emperor was revolting to us. Only cowards and animals surrender. We intend to fight until we are all killed. How degrading to put oneself into the hands of the enemy. To contemplate such a move was treason and such people should be arrested by the military police.

MRS TANIMOTO: Good day, may I introduce myself to you — I am Mrs Tanimoto. My husband is the Reverend Tanimoto, Kiyoshi Tanimoto. We were apart on that evening because my husband had insisted that I sleep in Ushida with my sister. Ushida is a suburb to the North of Hiroshima. It was very strange to be away from him even for a few days. But it was a wise decision and I could not disobey him. I don't suppose he liked getting his own breakfast. That night my sister and I had talked for a long time about the old days when we had lived at home. Once she had wanted to marry Mr Tanimoto but he chose me. She didn't speak to me for ages after that. In the morning I went back to the parsonage and began to do the housework with the housekeeper when:

MRS KAMAI: I am looking for my husband — have you seen him? Our baby is dead and he would like to see her once more — but soon it will be too late. He loved her very much. We were a nice little family — He and I our baby. Things were just right — have you seen him?

1ST SCIENTIST: In order to explain how a bomb works I'm afraid I must give a bit of a science lesson.

A bomb works because it is made to give off energy. But to understand this energy we must go right to the heart of the matter. Every object, every liquid, every gas is made up of one or more substances called matter. This matter is composed of elements and they in their turn can be divided into atoms.

2ND SCIENTIST: And that is what the scientists believed when in 1895 a German scientist discovered X-rays and saw on a luminous screen the very bones of his own hand. He had found how to produce rays that did not go round objects like light rays, but that could go through them.

1ST SCIENTIST: In 1896 a French scientist discovered that uranium has rays of inexhaustible radiation.

2ND SCIENTIST: In 1898 Marie Curie and her husband found after years of study and work that radium is a unique element which is a million times stronger than other radio-active elements.

1ST SCIENTIST: By 1900 X-rays were in frequent use in hospitals. Kings and commoners could see their own skeletons.

2ND SCIENTIST: X-rays were used to cure as well as discover illness. Skin disease, internal injury, malfunctions of the blood, cancer and skin TB all received the new therapy of X-rays and radium treatment. Then in 1902 a British scientist found that the element itself could change.

1ST SCIENTIST: This was a revelation in the world of science. Before, an element was itself and could be nothing else. But Rutherford said:

2ND SCIENTIST: 'Radio-active elements change, as a result of radiation, into other chemical elements.'

1ST SCIENTIST: And he could prove it. In 1911 this same man discovered that the atom —

2ND SCIENTIST: up till now the smallest chemical particle —

1ST SCIENTIST: contained inside itself a heart which he called a nucleus.

2ND SCIENTIST: In 1916 Rutherford split the nucleus.

All Things Are Matter

When we say 'What's the matter?'
We mean, 'What is wrong?'

Matter for the scientist
Is all things that exist
All life, all objects,
All material, all liquid.
All that moves with breathing
All that is still in death.
Fingers of transparent air
Mountains of ice
And rolling fish-filled sea.
All things are matter.

All things are matter
Earth, fire, water, air
Earth, fire, water, air
Earth, fire, water, air
All things are matter.

Matter is the essence of life
Matter is the decay of death
In the flaming sun, in the stars
Deep in the salt of the sea
Glistening, gleaming, in crystals of snow.

I am all of matter made
Eyelash, finger, bone displayed
Velvet flesh, body thin
Muscle, cartilage and skin
Curling hair, freckled brow
Ask me what's the matter now!

Matter is composed of elements.

If we take air
And inspect it and test it
We find in it elements
Of Oxygen, Hydrogen and Nitrogen.

Same form for water, earth and fire.

Elements are composed of molecules
A molecule is the smallest particle
Of any element or compound.

But the molecule is also
Divisable, made of atoms.

When fire burns slowly
Or ice is still

In the centre, in the heart
Is speed and heat
Beyond our understanding
Or our seeing.

HISTORIAN: A brief history of how a very big bomb was made.

GERMANY
1933: Hitler came to power. Many scientists then left Germany to go to America, Denmark and Britain. The British scientist Rutherford protested about the suppression of scientific freedom in Europe under Hitler.

1934: the end of free scientific research. Scientists not active in pro-German politics were suspect. Some were thrown out, others fled of their own accord.

1939: Germany started serious work on nuclear research. But she had not got the equipment. She was very worried about American progress in this field.

1941: A little progress.

1942: More progress. And Germany decides to use her nuclear knowledge for industry.

1945: Germany is defeated in the war.

AMERICA
1939: America was doing less actually than Germany imagined.

1940: The President appointed a team of scientists to work on atomic energy.

1943: Work was started on the problem of an atomic bomb. Many of the scientists, having fled from Germany, worked in hope that they might be privileged to drop a big bomb on Hitler himself.

1945: Two million dollars had been spent on the project, but Germany was defeated anyway. What should they do with the bomb? It had cost so much and could show the whole world how strong America was. They had enough knowledge and nuclear material for two uranium bombs and one plutonium bomb.

They worked by a new explosive principle. In the old chemical bombs a dissolution of matter makes the atoms form a different arrangement producing energy and heat. In the atomic bomb the nucleus itself inside the atom, is rearranged and this gives unimaginable heat plus radiation of deadly gamma rays.

US SECRETARY OF WAR: It is appalling that air raids on Japan should take place with no protest from the American people. I don't say the raids are wrong — only no one in this country protests about them.

PRESIDENT: Any bombing of civilian populations engaged in peaceful pursuits is unwarranted and contrary to the principles of law and humanity. We are not bombing for the sadistic pleasure of killing, but we are blowing to bits carefully selected targets like shipyards and factories.

HISTORIAN: After three years in the war American soldiers were dead on beaches and ditches around the world. Killing that was 'unwarranted' and against 'law and humanity' now in the words of the Federal Council of Churches was 'justifiable on Christian principles if it was essential to the successful conduct of a war that is itself justified'.

US SECRETARY OF WAR: This new bomb is too big for our planes, we'll have to use a British plane.

PRESIDENT: No. I want an American plane to deliver that bomb.

PILOT: Hiroshima then Kokura.

PRESIDENT: Destroy them. Don't pull your punches. Destroy them.

PILOT: Hiroshima, now Kokura.
Cloud! Can't see target area.
On to Nagasaki.

ALL: On to Nagasaki
Kokura is saved!

MRS MURATA: Good morning — I am Mrs Murata — I work at the vicarage as housekeeper — God knows when this wicked war will end. We must pray, pray everyday for the enemy's defeat. The Lord will surely not allow those Americans to win. How can cowards be victors? They do not approach us face to face — but kill us by distance. They hate to see our blood and our brains loosened from our body — but with a button to push — they can feel brave, even innocent. It is not important what I was doing that day, before the last bomb, the big one — I was thinking these thoughts and praying for the enemy's destruction.

MISS SASAKI: My name is Tashio Sasaki and I am a clerk at the East Asia Tin Works. That morning there was a lot to do before I even left the house. Akio, he is my brother, eleven months old, had a bad stomach and my mother had taken him to the Tamura Pediatric Hospital. She stayed with him there — so I had to do the breakfast for my father and my brothers and sister and me. Then I had to make meals for mother and Akio, that father would take to the hospital on his way to work. Hospitals don't provide meals in wartime. All this took until about seven, and then I had a forty minute bus ride in to work. I had a very responsible job — I was in charge of the personnel records in the factory. I suppose I was both lucky and unlucky really. I was a long way from the windows — but my chair was by some very large book cases — filled with very large books . . .

NARRATOR: Before they dare drop it, they had to test it, to make sure it was as destructive as they thought. After all, Japan was used to bombs — American ones — this one had to be big enough to force them into surrender. The test site was in Mexico, its code name — Trinity.

Code name — Trinity
Reminding us of holiness
Of the one in three of God.
Peace, cool churches
Forgiveness, humility
Self Sacrifice — Trinity.

Code name for destruction
Code name for
Jornada del Muerto
Journey of Death.
Beneath mountains called
The range of the Blood of Christ.

The valley was full
Of loneliness, waiting
for the experiments
Waiting for the news
of Trinity.

Hundreds of scientists were invited to join the team. They could bring their wives and their dogs. There were explosives experts, technical operators, mechanics, engineers, physicists, soldiers, airmen, canteen staff and security men. A man called Phillip Oppenheimer was in charge. Six feet tall, a gentle face with sapphire blue eyes and an aristocratic nose. He was a rare man, interested not only in science but in poetry and art too. When war came he had the idea of getting all the scientists of friendly nations together to work on this nuclear bomb project. When the idea was accepted he was put in charge.

The code name for the project was 'Manhatten Project' and it was very, very, very secret.

A: How would you like another job?

B: What have I done wrong?

A: Nothing.

B: What kind of a job?

A: Can't say.

B: Well, where is it?

A: Can't say.

B: East or West?

A: Sorry, my lips are sealed.

NARRATOR: Apart from work they played basketball, jazz and cards. They went for picnics and played jokes on each other.

One scientist, who played the banjo and only sometimes wore socks, worked out the combination to a safe where vital secret documents were kept. One night he opened it and left a little note. It said 'Guess who?!'

Tarantulas, cobras and rattlesnakes were not so much fun.

Work was started in January 1945.

By April things were going well, so well that all holidays were cancelled until after July.

Before the final test — four press releases were prepared to cover various results.

1. A loud explosion was reported today. There was no property damage or loss of life.
2. An extraordinary loud explosion was reported today. There was some property damage but no loss of life.
3. A violent explosion occurred today resulting in considerable property damage and some loss in life.
4. A mammoth explosion today resulted in widespread destruction of property and a great loss of life.

While no one could foresee exactly the result, they did not prepare a release to cover a non-explosion.

The medical people were worried that the glare might burn the eyes of the technicians.

The security people got very nervous towards the weeks of the test and the atmosphere of mystery and secrecy became greater and deadlier.

MRS CHURCH: Two hundred and twenty miles away Mrs Peggy Church had a sudden premonition. At dawn she locked the windows and the doors and thought with fear of a dream she had just had of seeing a strange and overwhelming wind — an invincible force that would destroy the earth.

A: The evening before the test one scientist broke down and was taken to a psychiatric ward.

B: And another said 'I'm scared witless, absolutely witless.'

NARRATOR: Five seconds before Zero a fire broke out. It was ignored — one small fire would not consume what was to come. Five, four, three, two, one. Zero.

DEATH: 'If the radiance of a thousand guns
Were to burn at once into the sky
That would be like the splendour of the Mighty One.
I am become Death
The shatterer of worlds.'

KATAOKA CHILDREN:
1. I had just learned in school about the Laotians and was telling my sisters. What did I tell you? Do you remember?

2. Um . . . they are Buddhists . . .

1. What else?

2. They are peace loving.

3. And in battle they are used to aiming their shots high in the expectation that their enemies will do the same.

1. That's right: then we were bombed.

DEATH: In natural circumstances it takes twenty-seven million years to produce a pound of Uranium 235.

In 1934 Marie Curie died. Officially, of pernicious anaemia. In fact the very marrow of her bones had died. She released the glowing powerful radium from its obscurity; had handled and touched it. It killed her.

In 1911, ten years after X-rays were first used in hospitals, fifty-four X-ray technicians died of cancer. Many radiography nurses were childless — not from choice.

In 1920, girls working in the Luminous Watch Factory in New

Jersey, USA fell ill, bleeding from the mouth. Seven died. They had licked the point of their paint brushes dipped in the luminous paint.

In 1945, one month after the Trinity test, a young scientist began to die. It took him a month. His hands were grossly swollen and the skin fell from his body in patches.

In May 1946 another scientist died of radiation poisoning. He too had touched this deadly thing. He lost his mind in a week and died nine days after in agony.

In August 1945, seventy-four thousand Japanese died.

MRS SUZUKI: My husband's name was Shinzo. He was a fisherman, very handsome, and we were quite happy although we hadn't much money. In fact Shinzo had to borrow to buy his boots and things for this last trip. That morning his boat was the first to go out for months. The Americans used to bomb the big fishing vessels, but so many people were hungry the captain thought it worth the risk. As usual the sailors were showing off to their girl friends, scrambling about on the rigging. Some of the girls were crying and some were being kissed. I waved to Shinzo and he came down on the pier. I expected a kiss myself or something — instead he slipped three thousand yen — that's about three or four English pounds, into my hand and asked me to try and get a job. Then he said 'Take care of your health', and he'd gone. I waved to him as the boat sailed away and then I started to go home. I just didn't know what to do next. How could I live on three thousand.

PILOT: Hiroshima, then Kokura.

PRESIDENT: Destroy them. Don't pull your punches.
Destroy them.

PILOT: Hiroshima, now Kokura.
Cloud! Can't see target area.
On to Nagasaki.

ALL: On to Nagasaki
Kokura is saved.

NARRATOR: And then in the clear warm morning, a single plane dropped its load on Hiroshima and later on Nagasaki.

DEATH: Out of the belly of the metal bird came the instruments of my pleasure: fire, flood, disease and poison.

Characters, repeat last paragraph of their speech.

NARRATOR: The Americans called the bomb 'Fat Man'.
He exploded above the city between eight and nine.
The blue sky was lost
In the white light of the monstrous fireball
It was a hundred times brighter than the sun
And as hot as the inside of the sun.
Then the sound came — unimaginable
For no one had ever heard a noise like this.
Then a wave of concussion
Flattened six thousand buildings.
At the centre of the bomb blast
Deadly gamma rays covered the earth.
The fireball sucked up millions of tons of dust
And shaped it into a great mushroom cloud.
Which hung above the city like a black cloud.

DEATH: The city burned for three days
And the embers smouldered for a week.

Bomb tableaux.

MRS NAKAMURA:	Oh the sky, the sky has fallen in.
MRS KAMAI:	My baby, where are you?
MISS SASAKI:	What is that thunder?
MISS TANIMOTO:	The earth has collided with a meteor.

MRS SUZUKI: A bomb has fallen directly on us.

MISS SASAKI: The ceiling is falling and the books — all the books.
Help me, they are crushing — I can't bear it —
The weight.

TOSHIO: Mother help me!

YAEKO: It hurts, Mother!

MYEKO *crying.*

MRS NAKAMURA: I'm coming. Don't worry, stop crying Myeko,
Lie still, I'm coming as fast as I can.

MRS TANIMOTO: Lord Jesus have pity on me. I don't want to die today. I'm not ready, let me go, have mercy, please, Jesus.

MRS SUZUKI: Shinzo, where are you? I've dropped the money — it's all gone. My arm hurts and I can't see. I want you here.

MRS KAMAI: I can't find my baby. Where are you darling — can't you make a noise and then I can reach you — where are you my darling?

DEATH: Fat Man, the bomb, was very clever. Not only did he spread poison and disease, but he killed all ranks of people — so doctors, nurses and firemen were also killed and injured and could not do their duties. Most of the fire was started when the wooden houses fell on cooking stoves and when electricity and gas mains exploded. Then it started to rain and as the tide rose in the river, people who had crawled to the cool water drowned. They were too weak to move.

MYEKO: Why is it night already? Why did our house fall down, what has happened?

MRS NAKAMURA: Be quiet Myeko and take my hand.

TOSHIO: I want to sit down.

YAEKO: I'm very tired.

MRS SUZUKI: My arm — help me — it is dead.

NARRATOR: Yaeko — your scarf — (*Makes a sling.*)

MRS SUZUKI: What has happened?

NARRATOR: I don't know — bombs I suppose.

TANIMOTO: How could it be? The whole city is destroyed. No, they have sprinkled us with gasoline and set light to it.

MRS SUZUKI: All my money's gone — my husband gave it to me.

KAMAI: Where is my husband? He must help me find her — she has gone.

She goes.

MISS SASAKI: My leg — help me, help me out.

MRS TANIMOTO: Mother, this lady has no leg.

NARRATOR: Help me shift her.

MISS SASAKI: The books are too heavy.

KATAOKA CHILDREN:
1. Excuse me please, can we stay with you?
2. We're lost.
3. It's your fault.
2. No it isn't — you should have kept up.
3. I was running as fast as I could. Anyway I want Mother.
1. Well she's lost too. Please excuse us quarrelling. But we've lost our mother, she went back for something we left in the house and we lost her in the crowd.
2. It was awful. Those people.
3. That man's face. And that woman in the gutter.
2. It wasn't a woman.
3. Yes it was.
1. Shut up — You couldn't tell anyway.

MRS TANIMOTO: I think you'd better sit down and rest. Your mother will probably come looking for you. Perhaps she's chasing after you now.

MRS KAMAI: Look I've found her — here she is.

MRS TANIMOTO: Oh, but your baby's . . .

MRS KAMAI: What's wrong with her?

MRS TANIMOTO: She's dead, dear.

NARRATOR: Let me see — Oh yes, look her mouth is full of dirt.

MRS KAMAI: It was when the house fell down — she was in the garden. I'm sure she'll be all right.

MRS SUZUKI: How can she be? — she's dead.

MRS KAMAI: No! She'll be all right in a bit.

1ST GIRL: Mother!

MRS MURATA: Mrs Tanimoto. Thank God you're alive. I would have been here sooner — but I went back for my shoes. Then I changed my mind. It's funny — yesterday they were so important to me — but today they don't matter.

MRS NAKAMURA: I know — I wanted to bring my sewing machine — but it's so heavy — and this is no time for sewing machines.

MRS KAMAI *sings to her baby.*

MRS SUZUKI: Stop that — it's already asleep — so deep that you'll never wake it.

MRS NAKAMURA: Ssssh!

MRS SUZUKI: Well how can she be so stupid! It's dead. Your child is dead.

MRS TANIMOTO: Don't you think you should put her down?

MRS NAKAMURA: Yes she really is dead. She wasn't strong enough.

MRS TANIMOTO: Now, let me have her.

MRS NAKAMURA: We'll put her

somewhere safe for you.

MRS KAMAI: No!

MRS SUZUKI: But she's dead.

MRS KAMAI: I know. But she's mine — not yours. Go away. You can't have her. I still want her — her father will want to say goodbye to her. Where is he? Have you seen him. He's such a good man — a soldier.

2ND GIRL: We saw some soldiers back near the river.

1ST GIRL: No.

3RD GIRL: But they were very burnt.

MRS KAMAI *screams.*

MRS SUZUKI: Put that corpse down. It'll smell soon.

She grabs the child — both grapple — MISS SASAKI *gets stepped on.*

MISS SASAKI: Oh God, my leg — it hurts. I thought it was numb — but it hurts.

DEATH: If the radiance of a thousand suns
Were to burst at once into the sky
That would be like the splendour of the Mighty One.
I am become Death
The shatterer of worlds!

MRS NAKAMURA: Have you heard the news?

MRS SUZUKI: What news?

MRS NAKAMURA: The war is over.

MRS SUZUKI: Don't say such a foolish thing.

MRS NAKAMURA: But I heard it over the radio myself. It was the Emperor's voice.

MRS SUZUKI: Oh . . . in that case.

MRS NAKAMURA: It was a wonderful blessing to hear his voice in person. We can be satisfied in such a great sacrifice.

MRS SUZUKI: It is disappointing . . .

MRS NAKAMURA: But we must follow his commandment with a calm spirit.

NARRATOR: Every year we climb to the top of this hill.

In 1945 an aeroplane passed over our city because it was covered with cloud. The plane carried a deadly atom bomb. It was scheduled to be dropped on us, but as the pilot's sights found only cloud he flew to another city and dropped his load there.

Every year we celebrate.

Good night.

They all go off, celebrating.

CLAM

Deborah Levy graduated from Dartington College of Arts. She is now a published poet and short story writer, and has collaborated with numerous visual artists on festival/gallery events. Her plays include *Pax* (Women's Theatre Group); *Dream Mamma* (Common Stock); and *Ophelia and the Great Idea* (Theatre Image-in-aire).

Sore

Remember this time.
When feelings hid in pinball machines
And the Inquisition shut down ideas.
When my emerald love dress
Refused to shake out its mothballs
And hung itself at dawn.

When angels ate their wings
Ethiopians ate their fists
The world threatened to eat itself
And truth found its syllables
Feathered and Tarred
And screaming in the bull rushes.

The time
We sat on time
Desperate for it to Hatch
And Cluck and make a Jump for life
Faith, that very ancient fruit
Trying to seed itself
Despite Everything.

Deborah Levy
1984

Characters
A MAN and a WOMAN double as:
ALICE and HARRY
VLADIMIR LENIN and NADIA KRUPSKAYA
DOCTOR and PATIENT

Set
Table
One large chair/one small chair
One large mug/one small mug
Fish tank

Clam was first presented by Blood Group, at the Oval House Theatre, London, on
25 April 1985, with the following cast:

ALICE/NADIA KRUPSKAYA/PATIENT	Miné Kaylan
HARRY/VLADIMIR LENIN/DOCTOR	Andrzey Borkowski

Directed by Anna Furse
Designed by Deborah Levy/Anna Furse

Scene One

In which ALICE *and* HARRY *discuss distance.*

> *Table.*
> *One large tin mug (Harry's).*
> *One small china cup and saucer (Alice's).*
> *One large chair (Harry's).*
> *One small chair (Alice's).*
> *Teapot.*
> *Large fish tank. Dominant.*

HARRY *wears a top hat with a dollar label stuck on it, and white kid gloves.*

ALICE *wears a scarlet puffed sleeved dress and black patent leather shoes.*

HARRY *pours tea. First a lot into the little china cup, and then a little into the big tin mug. He hands the cup and saucer to* ALICE.

ALICE: Thank you, Harry.

HARRY: I wish it was a pleasure, Alice. (*Lifting the mug.*) My fingers. Prematurely athritic. Sad.

ALICE: Your fingers probed my heart quite carelessly . . . in those days.

HARRY (*sipping tea*): But it's all very calm now.

ALICE: Yes.

HARRY: The joints. I have to crack each knuckle when I wake up in the mornings. I feel ridiculous. (*He laughs.*)

ALICE: Shame.

HARRY: Oh it's all right. Don't worry about me.

ALICE: I don't.

Both sip tea.

Cold.

HARRY: Lukewarm.

ALICE: But a comforting ritual nevertheless.

Pause.

HARRY: I suppose you'll want to know the time?

ALICE: I try not to think about it.

HARRY: It's very close indeed. (*He searches the table.*) Too close for comfort. I can taste it in my tea. (*He searches the teapot. He takes out a watch on a chain.*) Thought so. Two hands. That point to numbers. That measure out our day. I loved your hands.

ALICE: I've still got them.

HARRY: We forget . . . in the measuring out of moments . . . that there . . . there are . . .

ALICE: Clues.

HARRY: To explain distance.

They swop chairs.

A beginning and an end . . . measured out by these two hands . . . they could be East and West . . .

ALICE: They could be me and you . . .

HARRY: A beginning and an end that might not be . . .

ALICE: Resolved.

Pause.

Would you like a clam with your tea?

HARRY: It's just what I feel like right now.

ALICE *walks to the fishtank. She puts her arm into the water, swishes around.* HARRY *watches. He grimaces with every swish.* ALICE *triumphantly pulls out a clam. Brief interlude of* Schiller's 'Ode to Joy', *played very loud. She puts it on the small china plate and hands it to* HARRY.

Thank you, Alice.

ALICE: I wish it was a pleasure, Harry.

HARRY *cracks the clam.*

HARRY: There's not even the desire to hurt one another.

ALICE: No. (*The sound of the clam cracking.*) If I was far away from you, say we were separated by an ocean . . . any ocean . . . I would even write you letters.

HARRY: And I would reply. And take great care how I replied.

ALICE: I would look forward to that.

HARRY: I know you would.

ALICE: I might even think of you if I saw something in a shop I know you would like. Or send you a book. Or remember to tell you something someone had said to me. Or find some shoes . . . size nine . . . your size . . . and buy them for you . . . or a postcard with an image that would mean something to you . . . or look at a sculpture and imagine how you would see it . . .

HARRY: And it would not cause either of us to feel pain.

Pause.

There is a joke I have been meaning to tell you for some time. Ever since the Anthony Blunt affair.

ALICE: I'd like to share a joke with you.

Pause.

HARRY: How do moles go out together?

ALICE: How?

HARRY: On a blind date.

Pause.

ALICE: Harry?

HARRY: Yes?

ALICE: What would you do if something you really didn't want to see . . . flew two inches above your head?

HARRY: Duck.

Scene Two

In which LENIN *and* KRUPSKAYA *discuss lust.*
    Fish tank. Two 'fish' swim sublimely.
    A duck quacks off.

LENIN: Nadia Krupskaya! Why do you keep your husband waiting like this?

NADIA (*off*): I am plucking a duck, Vladimir.

LENIN (*pacing*): A duck? My Nadia is plucking a duck . . . and I am gathering my thoughts in order to address two thousand spirit-gutted comrades in five minutes . . . a carefully drawn up plan on how best reform can be achieved in the sixth wing of the . . .

NADIA *enters wearing a head-dress of feathers. She dances a brief Russian dance. Shouts of Hey! Hey!*

(*He staggers.*) You want to give me a revolutionary heart attack? My wife dressed like a bourgeois peacock . . .

NADIA: An ideologically sound *duck*, Vladimir.

LENIN: Strutting before my far-seeing and penetrating eyes like a typsy czarina . . . *Nadia*!

NADIA: Kiss me Vladimir.

LENIN (*collecting himself*): I will shake your hand in a friendly manner. And then you will remove your foolish finery and accompany your husband like an honest wife . . . instead of a clucking foul who has lost all reason.

NADIA: *Oh Vladimir!* That our hearts might be banners of *unreason* just once. For they are good hearts . . . pumping victorious and glorious as our machines . . . a little lustful oil . . . Vladimir . . .

LENIN *strides to the fish tank. He takes a mouthful of water. He gargles. Spits. The water turns red.*

LENIN: I wash your mouth out for you, Nadia. You make a mockery of the struggle . . . of science . . . for what is scientific is truth and can never be criticised . . .

NADIA: Let me *feel* science then, Vladimir . . . dab science on my nipples, on my period pains, on my pulse points . . . on the small of my back . . .

Pause.

LENIN: Nadia. You are not well. I feel compassion and will be tender with you for one minute. (*He takes a watch on a chain from his pocket, checks it, puts it back, walks to her.*)

NADIA: A little closer, Vladimir.

He embraces her stiffly.

Aaaaah. Vladimir . . . you have strong arms for a man who works so much with his head . . . Vladimir . . . if . . . if . . . just once we could maybe pack a picnic and eat black bread in the pine forest . . . alone with the beatings of our hearts . . . or sit on the balcony drinking lemon tea . . . perhaps playing chess . . . and although we were silent . . . it would be . . . an involved silence . . . you might even cook me something . . . soup or a little salt beef with horse radish . . . and we would sing our songs together . . . you might even loose yourself a little . . . intoxicate your clear thinking with the black sea smell of my hair . . .

LENIN (*pulls away from her*): I prefer the honest smell of dung . . . the gentle sigh of dialectic. You are in need of re-education. I am looking at a sick woman.

NADIA: *Look* at me then.

He looks at her piercingly.

S W O O N!

LENIN: Swoon? You are asking a man who has rocked the world with the most significant social change this century has witnessed . . . to swoon?

NADIA: Yes.

Pause.

Fucking swoooooon will you?

Pause.

S W O O O O O N!!!

LENIN (*takes out a red hanky, wipes his brow*): I . . . I . . . I . . .

He staggers.

NADIA: MORE!

LENIN: I . . . I . . . I . . . (*Staggering more.*) What do you want from me Nadia?

NADIA: PASSION!

LENIN (*staggers to the fish tank*): What . . . what you understand subjectively as love . . . does not matter . . .

NADIA: *Love*? Who's talking about love?

LENIN: What matters is the objective logic of class relations in affairs of love . . .

NADIA *leaps towards him. She sticks his head under the water of the fish tank. She holds him under.*

NADIA: Then I will have to find a young comrade to explore this 'objective logic' with . . . for short-lived passion is more poetic and pure than the dry kisses of doctrine . . . we will explore ideology between the legs and in the arm pit . . . we will . . .

LENIN (*surfacing*): Nadia? Why do you put goldfish in the samovar?

NADIA: It was a wicked aberration of the imagination, Vladimir.

LENIN: I frown like the furrows we plough in our frozen fields, my wife. We are talking about revolution not imagination.

NADIA: Imagination, Vladimir, like revolution, is the last resort of the under-privileged.

LENIN: You are a sick woman. I look upon you as a doctor would his patient.

Scene Three

In which DOCTOR *and* PATIENT *explore non-sense.*
  The PATIENT *is horizontal.*

PATIENT: Doctor, I am a sick woman.

DOCTOR: You say you have pains in your stomach, Patient?

PATIENT: The pains in my stomach are imperialism, Doctor.

DOCTOR: Uh huh.

PATIENT: I need to be rehabilitated.

DOCTOR: Locate your symphony and begin.

PATIENT: Day by day my discerning senses are being numbed. I have come to the conclusion this is not a personal disability but an international conspiracy.

DOCTOR (*quickly holds up four fingers*): How many internationals am I holding up?

PATIENT: Your mother, grandmother, sister and wife.

The lights dim. Spot on DOCTOR. *He addresses the audience.*

DOCTOR: Gentlemen, the case I have to place before you today is a curious one. Not only does the patient insist she is a woman, she insists she is a Russian woman. When she continued to insist I stuck a needle through her forehead. She seems genuinely distressed by the state of the world and often attempts a political analysis of contemporary world affairs. As this does show evidence of thought and is plainly a danger to herself, I placed clamps on her wrists and negotiated short electric spasms through her skull by placing electric wires on her forehead. The patient does not seem to worry in the least about her surroundings.

Spot switches to PATIENT.

PATIENT: Dear Alice, he told me I was insane and irrational. Then he stuck a needle through my forehead. Then he put clamps on my wrists. Then he put electric wires on my temple and burnt some of my hair. Love, Nadia.

PATIENT *and* DOCTOR *resume treatment.*

DOCTOR: Do you have a particular association with helicopters?

PATIENT: The army.

DOCTOR: Are you frightened of the army?

PATIENT: I'm frightened of you too.

The DOCTOR *plucks a feather from her head-dress. She winces.*

Do you think we were born cruel doctor?

DOCTOR: Yes.

They both cry loudly and inconsolably. They suddenly stop.

Do you think we were born kind, loving and full of need, Patient?

PATIENT: Yes.

They both laugh loudly and hollowly.

DOCTOR: So tell me something I haven't heard before?

Scene Four

In which ALICE *and* HARRY *find clues. Darkness.*
The sound of water splashing.
ALICE *and* HARRY *sit by the fish tank which is full of all kinds of objects: ie, a brush, comb, shoes, a bible, an orange, cigarettes, a necklace, the complete works of Shakespeare, a Union Jack, sweets . . . etc.*
They take it in turns to fish things out of the tank and name them.

HARRY: Oh look! I've just found a dinosaur's knee cap!

ALICE: And I've found a dinosaur's elbow!

HARRY: Is it a knuckle?

ALICE: No it's a gas chamber.

HARRY: Tell me a story, Alice.

ALICE: You're bound to tell me you've heard it all before.

HARRY: Then I'll find it reassuring. Is this an apartheid?

ALICE: No it's a fathom. Which reminds me. Last week I went for a walk across twenty-five miles of a beach forbidden to me . . . decided to risk the radio-active herbage seaweed string plastic . . .

HARRY: Think I've found an etcetera . . .

ALICE: No. That's a Cumbria. Or it could be a clandestine.

Pause.

Do you know what I found there, Harry?

HARRY: Mohammedanism?

ALICE: Extinct creatures. Scattered across the rocks and shingle . . . creatures that would never geographically survive there . . . I found things under shrubs . . . that should never have been there . . .

HARRY: Pearls?

ALICE: A Tapir . . . a bit like a lizard . . . all the way from Venezuela . . . perhaps Ecuador or Columbia . . . its mouth open and under its tongue little bits of decaying fruit and shoots from trees . . . as if it had predicted its own extinction . . . a *Yak* . . . Harry I found a dead yak . . . all the way from the Tundra . . . lying on its back by a bush . . . further on . . . nearer the rock pools I found a Rhino . . . its head was severed from its body . . . the horn removed . . . piles of excrement scattered across the reeds . . . I kept walking . . . must have done about eight miles by now . . . saw something peeping out of the sand . . . an eye . . . the pupil was white so I knew whatever it was was blind . . . I dug with my hands . . . the sand soft as butter . . . an *antelope* Harry . . . beautiful black patches on its forehead . . . it had been shot there too . . . the bullet still lodged in the flesh and bone . . .

HARRY: Is this an idiosyncracy?

ALICE: Looks like a broody. (*Pause.*) The sea was very calm that day . . . grey green . . . I stood close to the shore enjoying the air and wind . . . bent down to pick up a stone to throw out . . . saw the last of the creatures . . . there by my feet . . . I remember reading about it . . . oh years before I met you . . . a *Tuatara* . . . like a small dragon with tiny stings on its chest . . . known as the sting carrier . . . and by it . . . a whole clutter of unhatched eggs . . . some buried in the mud . . . covered with salt crystals . . . they just lay there . . . so hopeful . . . paper thin shells . . . I put my hand to my head and found some of my hair was falling out . . . and I began to wonder Harry, whether I was becoming extinct . . . put my hands down my pants . . . discovered blood on my fingers . . . just a little . . . nothing to worry about.

HARRY: I'd like to make a sculpture of you, Alice.

ALICE: I vomited into the sea . . . quite suddenly . . . and I had this *vision* Harry . . . watching the patterns my vomit made with the waves . . . The whole of Eastern Europe . . . much of it extinct . . . came in with the tide . . . Poland . . . Latvia . . . Lithuania . . . Hungary . . . Czechoslovakia . . . dropped on our poisoned shores . . . and thousands of people ran out to look . . . children with buckets and spades . . . adults in sun hats . . . teenagers with radios hugged to their ears . . . shop keepers . . . ice-cream sellers . . . all stood in silence just looking . . . for a long time . . . until some began to touch and smell . . . turned Hungary on its side and began to feel it . . . a little boy kissed the Ukraine . . . his father smacked him . . . a woman in a bikini put Poland on her belly . . . sighed . . . placed her lover's hand there too . . . an old man buried his head in Lithuania and wept . . . And then I saw further out . . . just a speck on the sea, *India* . . . stranded . . . babies with khol-blacked eyes gashed themselves on the rocks . . . a yoghurtmaker's ladle bobbed up and down . . . lillies . . . cucumber . . . fennel . . . aniseed . . . churned with the waves . . .

HARRY: I've just found another rabbit hole.

ALICE: And I another laxative.

HARRY: Is it evangelical?

ALICE: Nor is it a lake.

Pause.

Kiss me Harry.

Pause.

HARRY: You see, Alice, if you walked twenty-five miles along a radioactive beach, it would not be a good idea to kiss you.

Very loud and brief rendering of 'Ode to Joy'.

Scene Five

In which DOCTOR and PATIENT discuss 'The Enemy'.
    The DOCTOR is eating a carrot fished up from the tank in the previous scene.

PATIENT: It's not a very good idea to eat that carrot.

DOCTOR: Oh?

The DOCTOR continues to eat with more relish.

Why's that?

PATIENT: It was washed up on the shores of a radioactive beach.

DOCTOR: I see.

PATIENT: It might send you a bit funny.

DOCTOR: Really?

A pause as he chews and thinks.

The diagnosis? I think you are severely disillusioned. Bitter. Twisted. Titter.

Bwisted. Twitter. Blistered. Bwittered. Twitterered.

This can go on for some time as he goes 'funny'.

The prescription? Years of imprisonment. Phone tapping. Mounted police. Electric shocks. I suppose you want to know the time?

PATIENT: I try not to think about it.

DOCTOR: Tea time. (*He picks objects up from the floor.*) So who cares about the cholesterol? Will you partake in a petit-bourgeois?

PATIENT: MAY THE PETIT-BOURGEOIS DROWN IN THEIR SWEET SOUTH AFRICAN SHERRIES!!!

The DOCTOR hands her another.

PATIENT: IN THEIR PALE EAU DE COLOGNES!!!

The DOCTOR hands her another.

PATIENT: IN THEIR CUT GLASS BOWLS OF TRIFLE!!!

Pause.

DOCTOR: I've treated thousands of patients like you.

PATIENT (*quiet*): When the next war comes to be written up doctor . . . it will be known . . . quite simply . . . as the war men fought against women.

DOCTOR (*mouth full*): Do you hate me, Patient?

Scene Six

In which ALICE and HARRY discuss aesthetics.
    HARRY in a big chair.
    ALICE in a little chair.

ALICE: Are you still fond of me, Harry?

HARRY: If I was to involve myself in relation to an object, let's say a sculptural involvement as I am a sculptor . . . and was asked to choreograph myself into one of my exhibitions . . . I could do a number of things. I could stand in relation to shape, weight, texture, height, scale, colour. I would have to decide whether I wanted to make my body shape similar to the object . . . or contrast myself with it. Feeling and pychology would not come into the equation. Unless I was interested in descriptive gesture. But then I'm not interested in being profound or polemic or a catalyst for social change. Merely presenting a sequence of abstracted movement.

They swop chairs.

ALICE: If you were talking to me about love I would listen to you and while you were talking I would see that you were observing the angle of my hand in relation to the window frame, or the poised fingers of a woman smoking a cigarette in relation to the blue curtains, or the plastic milk carton in relation to the porcelain jar from Britanny containing mead which being very sweet you might contrast with three withered lemons juxtaposed by chance at an interesting angle in relation to an old woman with withered breasts whose ankles might be interesting in relation to the four legs of the green straw chair . . . not forgetting the window frame in relation to the whole composition.

They swop chairs.

HARRY: And would you stop listening to me?

ALICE: I would stop listening to the words you were saying.

They swop chairs.

HARRY: Does that mean you would involve yourself with the politic of my body?

ALICE: I would involve myself with the politic of your evasion.

HARRY: Then we are in a state of concord. For I would be interested in

peripheral relationships and you would be forced to relate to me peripherally.

Pause.

ALICE: Would you like a clam without your tea, Harry?

HARRY: Thank you, Alice. That's just what I feel like right now.

Scene Seven

In which DOCTOR and PATIENT discuss science.

DOCTOR (*plucking feathers*): She loves me, she loves me not, she loves me, she loves me not, she loves me . . .

PATIENT: And then doctor, by chance . . . you found a metaphor to describe your own schizophrenia . . . you split an atom.

Scene Eight

In which HARRY gives an interview. HARRY *sits alone. Tea set laid out for one. He wears hat and gloves as in Scene One. He looks straight out.*

VOICES OFF:
    1: Lights.
    2: Yes.
    1: Sound.
    2: Yes.
    1: Camera.
    2: Yes.
    1: Fire!

HARRY: I'm sorry Alice got shot. (*He pours tea.*) But I'm glad an American soldier shot her and not a Brit. No, I don't think she had a death wish. In fact she was pregnant. Yes, she was a close friend of mine and I'll miss her. I am at the moment exhibiting my most recent sculptures and have called the composition 'Women at War'. It explores this whole question of civil disobedience. You'll find the address of the gallery in most respectable arts listings. Since the tragic incident I have been commissioned to write a short essay on the subject for an eminent publishing house. This will come out in July and can be purchased at most respectable book shops.

Pause.

It feels strange drinking tea alone.

He sips tea.

She would have made a very good mother. Poor Alice and her unhatched egg.

Scene Nine

In which NADIA KRUPSKAYA *and* VLADIMIR LENIN *discuss what is to be done.*
LENIN *paces the floor. He is irate.*

LENIN: NADIA KRUPSKAYA!

Pause.

NADIA!

NADIA (*off*): I am plucking a poet, Vladimir.

LENIN: A poet? HA! I suppose he tells you the sky is yellow and the grass pink . . . whispers sweet pumpkin cake verse in your ear . . .

NADIA: We have a strictly non-verbal relationship, Vladimir.

LENIN: HA! Because if he opened his mouth . . . what would come out . . . a sugar lump? A little philosophy . . . something he picked up on a tram? Borschst without Beetroot. Nadia! Come to your husband!

NADIA: C.O.M.I.N.G.

LENIN *takes out a watch on a chain. He paces.*

LENIN: Why does my heart beat like this? Very fast. All week I have felt . . . tearful . . . my dreams are unspeakable . . . one gets the feeling . . . there is so little time . . . time for

what, I ask? My shoes pinch . . . twice I have loosened my collar, my lip twitches . . . hands shake . . . It is not good for the morale of my people to show fear . . . weakness . . . and then I think . . . to acknowledge the fear . . . maybe . . . to voice the unspeakable . . . might be a good thing . . . to have achieved so much . . . so huge a task . . . so many sacrifices . . . Our people . . . opened their hearts to change . . . and it happened . . . we built ourselves a future . . . out of nothing . . . problems . . . many problems . . . we said we could not achieve everything at once . . . we made mistakes . . . and the West laughed at us . . . relished our every stumble . . . trod on our young bones . . . but against all the odds . . . considerable odds . . . we grew . . . put our faith and blood in what was right . . . I had vision and they came with me . . . they had muscle and they used it . . . and now to think . . . our great bear . . . once half starved, limping, chained . . . now with a good coat of fur, bright eyes, Russian eyes . . . might not . . . bear cubs . . . or will give birth to mutant beasts with three heads . . . is this a tear Vladimir? . . . am I weeping like a child? . . . to think we conquered feudalism . . . slavery . . . for this . . .

NADIA, *enters, shy, tender.*

NADIA: Vladimir?

LENIN: Nadia.

Pause. They want to embrace each other but can't. LENIN *takes out a red hanky wipes his eyes.*

LENIN: What is to be done, Nadia?

Pause.

NADIA: We will have to teach ourselves to sing again. But first, Vladimir . . . we will dance together . . .

He walks towards her. Lightly embraces her. They slowly, shyly, awkwardly start to dance.

LENIN (*shy*): You will have to teach me the steps.

NADIA: And you will have to listen.

Pause.
Faint twinkle of the 'Internationale' on the piano.

NADIA (*soft*): Oh Vladimir. All this madness . . . all this *sch-mozzle* . . . all this bad stuff . . . we must try and undo the evil spell . . . to clip the wings of the greedy eagle . . . of birds of prey . . . swooping down on all that is good . . . once and for all . . .

VLADIMIR: How . . . my love with red lips, red heart, my love whose eyes are lined with sociological tide marks . . .?

NADIA (*laughs*): So you have become a poet in ten seconds . . . Vladimir . . .

VLADIMIR (*a little carried away*): My love whose spirit sparkles like snow on the Kremlin's roof top . . . whose brain spins like a top on the skulls of philistines . . . ha . . . I am getting a taste for poetics am I not? . . . I will speak to the printers . . . maybe a slim volume . . . 'Dialectical Ditties for my Darling' . . .

NADIA (*dancing*): One two . . . two three . . . the next step, Vladimir . . . must be as imaginative as it is political . . .

LENIN *stumbles. She yanks him up.*

Alice, my British sister, I made a wreath for you . . . out of mint and lemon leaves . . . I want you to know that you and your unborn child have a place in the hearts of all Russian women. (*Pause.*) If we are to be saved Vladimir . . . we will have a marriage . . .

LENIN: But we *are* married Nadia . . .

NADIA: A marriage of science and intuition.

LENIN: Have you become a Catholic these days, Nadia?

NADIA (*laughs*): I worship no gods Vladimir. If I had my way I would put them all to sleep and waken the goddesses . . . we have become orphans, my husband . . . and need to solder all that is disconnected . . . to re-learn intelligence . . . one one . . . two . . . three . . . we will have to create *want*.

LENIN: I want to empty my bladder Nadia . . .

NADIA: The *want* to acquire a sound knowledge of each others needs . . .

LENIN: Nadia . . .

NADIA: The want of each other. Vladimir. At this moment in our history . . . we are very very ugly.

LENIN: My mother always told me I had a determined profile and faultless eyes.

NADIA: Your mother was being kind. In certain lights you look like a pig.

LENIN: Nadia . . .

NADIA: But I love you all the same. I have even grown used to the lice in your beard.

LENIN: I swear by Pushkin . . .

NADIA: Tomorrow you will enrole for an art class at the institute . . . under the surreal tutorship of Pearlie Popova . . . and I for my first physics lesson. That is what is to be done Vladimir . . . and you have wet yourself. And that is a beginning.

The dance continues.
Lights fade.
The audience should leave in half light.

KEEPING BODY AND SOUL TOGETHER

For Tanya

Stephen Lowe has written widely for the theatre. His plays include *Comic Pictures* (Scarborough, 1976); *Sally Ann Hallelujah Band* (Nottingham Playhouse Theatre Roundabout, 1977); *Touched* (Nottingham Playhouse, 1977; Royal Court Theatre, 1981; joint winner of the George Devine Award); *The Ragged Trousered Philanthropists* (Joint Stock, 1978; Half Moon, London, 1983); *Glasshouses* (later retitled *Moving Pictures,* Royal Court Theatre Upstairs, 1981); *Tibetan Inroads* (Royal Court, 1981); *Stars* and *Strive* (performed as a double-bill at Sheffield Crucible Studio, 1983); *Seachange* (Riverside Studios, 1984); and *Keeping Body and Soul Together* (Royal Court Theatre Upstairs, 1984). For television he has written *Shades* and *Cries from a Watchtower.* He was a resident playwright at Dartington College of Arts from 1978-1982, and at Riverside Studios in 1984.

Keeping Body and Soul Together

The fear of the holocaust permeates every thought, feeling, and breath we take, like a cancer. And often like a cancer we dare not consciously face up to it, and admit its possible intrusion into our way of life. Most critically, if not faced, it separates us from a creative belief in a future and increases our sense of alienation and lack of power.

This comedy/love story came from my attempt to follow that fear into the most private, the most personal aspects of our lives. I hope you *enjoy* it.

Stephen Lowe
1985

Keeping Body and Soul Together is set in the present day in the small front room of a terraced house in a small Northern town.

An earlier two-act version of this play was first performed at the Royal Court Theatre Upstairs on 19 November 1984, with the following cast:

KATE	Janette Legge
BOB	Clive Russell
TREVOR	Philip Whitchurch

Directed by Susan Todd
Designed by Sue Plummer
Lighting by Leo Leobovici
Sound by Andy Pink

Dark.

Country & Western music: Loretta Lyn singing 'Coalminer's Daughter'. In between tracks the additional sound of heavy breathing.

A COALMINER, *surfaces from a trap in the centre of the stage. The light from the pit helmet reveals elements of the 'living-room' of a terraced house – a divan, a table with an old typewriter, a shelf of potted cacti, a kid's battered (stuffed) leopard, and a somewhat incongrous cheap wardrobe. The* MINER *pushes a large plastic bag into the room, and disappears. This is repeated twice, until the* MINER *scrambles out, switches on a standard lamp, and strips down to bra and pants, while swaying slightly to the rhythm of the music.* KATE *replaces her protective clothing on hooks on the underside of the trapdoor. Her face and hands are covered in a thick layer of mud.*

She finally hears the knocking on the hall door, and, panicking, loads one sack into an old pram, slings a duvet over to disguise the others, closes the trap, grabs a dressing-gown and slides the bolt open on the door, to reveal –

BOB, *dressed in a cheap but clean suit and tie. He stands, transfixed by the sheer volume of the music. She switches the record off. This however still leaves the heavy breathing clearly emanating from two speakers in the centre of the room.*

KATE (*crossing to turn them down*): So I can hear the kids.

BOB: Ah, ye', right.

She turns to face him, and he then steps back, startled.

KATE (*alarmed*): What's up?

BOB: No, no, nothing, Mrs Sinclair, only . . .

KATE: Wha', is it the dressing-gown? Well, I'm not well, you see, I have a chest infection. (*She coughs.*) Just plannin' to rub Vic on it, (*she breathes deeply.*) and then to bed. I go to bed early. That's why I said don't disturb me after the kids were asleep.

He nods, tensely. There is clearly still something disturbing him. She checks herself in the wardrobe mirror.

Ah! Yes, you're probably wondering about the . . . er . . .

BOB: No, no, no. Not really. Well . . .

KATE: Mudpack. Greasy pores. Wi' having kids. Too many chips. (*Notices her hands.*) And fish fingers.

BOB: Right. (*Pause.*) I had acne, through eating chips. Mind you, that were a long time ago. (*Nervously checks his watch.*) Good Lord, is that the time? Half past eight already? Well, I won't keep you up. Thank you very much. Sorry.

He begins backing out.

KATE: But what was it you wanted, Mr Huddlestone?

BOB (*backing out*): No, sleep. Get your beauty sleep. Another time.

KATE: But it must be important. You an't bothered me before.

BOB: And I don't intend to bother you now.

KATE: You're not bothering me!

BOB: Are you sure?

KATE (*tensely*): You're not bothering me at all. Please, sit down.

KATE *retrieves a plate and breadknife that he accidentally treads on. He sits, uncomfortably, on the divan. Silence. He stares at the lumpy duvet.*

KATE: Have you a problem sleeping?

BOB: Well, I woun't –

KATE: Are you too cold? I used to have an electric up there, 'for I got the duvet. I find duvets are best, don't you? My husband hated it, used to set off his allergy. But I've allers been fond of them. (*Sighs.*) Listen, you can have the electric. I've never trusted it. Never felt safe with hot plugs in bed. It's somewhere in the basement, no, I mean the attic. I can dig it out.

(*Pause.*) Eh, that looks as though that's what I've been doing, dun't it?

BOB: Pardon?

KATE: Diggin'.

She laughs. BOB *nods and tries to join in. Silence. She pops the plate and knife in the pram, and moves to the door to show him out.*

KATE: So if you can survive tonight —

BOB: What?

KATE: I'll get it down first thing in the morning. Can't have my lodger freezin', can I?

BOB (*stands*): Yes, thank you, but it won't the electric blanket I wanted.

KATE: Well, I coun't gi' up me duvet.

BOB: Oh, no, I won't suggesting that. In fact, it won't about the bed I came down.

KATE: Well, why you been goin' on about it?

BOB: I don't —

KATE: Is it the kids? Do they still keep charging in? I burnt Adam's plastic hammer, I swear it.

BOB: Oh, there was no need. I had to get up anyway.

KATE: They're still not used to me not bein' in there.

BOB: They're no bother, honest.

KATE: Well, what's wrong wi' the room?

BOB: It's a very pleasant room.

KATE: It's the only one gets the morning sun.

BOB: That dun't bother me too much.

KATE: Oh, I thought you'd like it.

BOB: Well, it wakes me up. I like to get me sleep.

KATE: I don't see I can do much about that.

BOB: No, no, I din't expect you could. I won't complaining, in any way. No, it were more a favour I come to ask you.

KATE (*coldly*): A favour? What sort of favour?

BOB (*with difficulty*): Well, I woun't want you to think after what you said about not disturbing you down here, that I was trying to muscle in on —

KATE: Muscle in?

BOB: Only I've got this rather unexpected meeting, with a . . . friend tonight, and I thought better than us being cramped up there, having to bounce up and down on the bed (*Laughs.*) Well, that you might see your way clear to —

KATE: Bounce up and down on the bed? (*Pause.*) Look, Mr Huddlestone, if you want to bring a woman back here —

BOB: Oh, no, it in't a woman. Far from it. Quite the reverse.

KATE (*Pause*): Oh, I see. Well, don't misunderstand me. I've got nothing against such relationships between men. In fact the more you lot take up wi' each other and leave us women alone the better. But I really don't see I can have your friend muscling in on my room because yours is too small.

BOB (*consumed with embarrassment*): Excuse me, Mrs Sinclair. It's not like that. I'm not like that. It's a business meeting. He's a business colleague not a . . .

Silence.

KATE: Oh, I am sorry. I din't mean to offend you.

BOB: Misunderstandings easily happen. (*Pause.*) It's just we have to have a very short meeting, and it seemed my bedroom wasn't perhaps the ideal venue.

KATE: Well, coun't you meet him in a pub?

BOB: Well, that would be very nice, ye', but you see in planning you have to be very confidential, particularly in the beginning. Don't want folk to start panicking unnecessarily.

KATE (*panicking*): Panicking? About what?

BOB: Well, about plans, you know.

KATE: What sort of planning are you into, Mr Huddlestone?

BOB (*evasive*): Just normal town and country planning.

KATE: What would you plan in this town? The council don't have the money to white wash a lav ne' mind —

BOB: Mainly country planning.

Silence.

KATE (*pause*): In the country. Is it to do wi' the airbase then?

BOB (*confused*): Well, possibly, perhaps.

KATE: What you planning there? What are them Yanks up to now?

BOB: I din't say it was the airbase, specifically.

KATE: That's all the countryside there is round here.

BOB: Is it? I an't seen a great deal.

KATE: Well, you don't get out much, do you? I had thought you'd be out all the time, goin' round measuring wi' your triangles and your theosophytes —

BOB: Pardon?

KATE: You an't even got a car.

BOB: Ye', well, that's a common misconception, Mrs Sinclair. Most of planning's done up here, you know.

He taps his forehead. Silence.

Well, what do you think?

KATE *is clearly not pleased.*

KATE: When is this top secret meeting?

BOB: I'm afraid it's now.

KATE: Now?

BOB: These things are always last minute.

I only got the letter meself this morning.

KATE: That official looking letter?

BOB: Oh, you noticed that, did you?

KATE: Not really, no. Bit short notice this is.

BOB: Can't let the grass grow under your feet.

KATE: Why din't you ask me before?

BOB: Well, you were tied up wi' your children, and . . .

KATE: This in't going to be a regular occurrence, is it?

BOB: Just a one off, I promise you.

KATE (*sighs*): It dun't leave me much time to tidy up. It looks like a tip.

BOB: Not at all. And anyway he won't be here long enough to notice.

She moves the toys away.

KATE: These government fellows don't miss a trick.

BOB: It's really very good of you.

KATE: I have to get this mud off 'fore it cracks me face wide open, and I end up looking like an earthquake instead of the usual swamp.

BOB: You do yourself an injustice.

KATE: I know.

BOB (*nervously*): Exactly.

BOB *is saved from her withering glance by the front door bell.*

I'll get it.

KATE: Let me just slip upstairs first.

She quickly gathers some clothing from the untidy wardrobe.

BOB: It's very good of you.

KATE (*without enthusiasm*): My pleasure.

She switches off the tannoy, and leaves. BOB leaves. Off-stage can be heard greetings and BOB guiding the visitor into the lounge. The MAN enters first. He surveys the room. As

*civil servants go he is straightforward
and amiable. Clearly a lot that he sees
on the job might depress him, but he is
apparently not without belief in his
work.* BOB *notices he is staring at
some underwear* KATE *has dropped
by the wardrobe.*

BOB: This in't my room. Obviously. It's
my landlady's.

VISITOR: Mrs Sinclair.

BOB: You know her, do you?

VISITOR (*mildly*): Oh, yes, we know
her. How are the children keeping?

BOB: All right.

The VISITOR *stares at the pram.*

BOB: It won't take long all this, will it?

VISITOR: No.

BOB: Only as I told your mate on the
counter, she dun't know I'm on the
dole, or she woun't have let me the
room. I 'ad to make up a hell of a cock
and bull story to get her out the road
as it is.

The VISITOR *crosses to the table and
opens his briefcase to take out* BOB's
file.

VISITOR: I understand. What'll you do if
you can't find work round here?

BOB: Move on again, I guess.

VISITOR: Where to? There's a lot of you
in the same boat.

BOB: I know.

VISITOR (*sympathetically*): Ye' well,
we'll help as much as we can. I know
folk see us as Thatcher's task force,
but we are concerned with the
welfare of our clients.

He studies the file.

BOB: Will you want to see me bedroom?

VISITOR: I think I can imagine that.

BOB *is clearly on edge.*

BOB (*nervous*): It's such a funny time for
a visit.

VISITOR: For some people it's the crack
of dawn.

BOB: Shiftworkers?

VISITOR (*smiling*): Moonlighters. Of one
sort or another. They keep us on our
toes.

BOB: I can imagine.

VISITOR (*indicating the divan*): Is that
one of those that pulls out into a
double bed?

BOB: Ye'.

VISITOR: How do you know that?

BOB (*confused*): Well, they all do, don't
they?

VISITOR: Do they?

BOB (*pause*): Here, hang on. I know you
blokes have to investigate everything
but if you're makin' out that there's
some . . . you know . . .

VISITOR: No. What?

BOB: Well, that I'm in some way . . .
er . . . with Mrs Sinclair.

VISITOR (*smiling*): Oh, no, no, nothing
was further from my mind than you
were co-habitting and making a false
claim. Anyway, I haven't come to
investigate you, but to offer you a bit
of advice.

BOB: What sort of advice?

*He ignores him and stares into the
pram.*

VISITOR: What on earth is this?

BOB: It's a pram, innit?

VISITOR: No, I mean, inside the pram.

BOB *reluctantly crosses over.*

BOB: Well, it looks like a plastic bag.

VISITOR: And what do you think
is inside the bag?

BOB: I dunno.

The VISITOR *opens it up.*

BOB: Here, I don't think you're entitled
to —

He pulls out a handful of soil.

VISITOR: Soil!

BOB: Wha'?

VISITOR: Is she in the habit of taking a pramfull of soil walkies?

BOB: I dunno. I don't know ought about her.

The VISITOR follows the trail of soil towards the duvet.

VISITOR: Curiouser and curiouser.

He pulls back the duvet to reveal the remaining sacks.

VISITOR: Would you care to make a guess as to why she's hoarding soil?

BOB: Perhaps she's worried about flooding.

VISITOR: At the top of this hill? Even Noah wouldn't bother to build an ark up here.

BOB *shrugs and sits on the divan.*

VISITOR: Not something that arouses your curiosity, Mr Huddleston?

BOB: If you want to know, ask her.

VISITOR: And you think she'll tell me the truth?

BOB: Why shun't she?

VISITOR (*sighs; pause*): You like to think the best of people, don't you, Mr Huddllestone?

BOB: I just mind my own business.

VISITOR: So do I. (*Pause. He sits by BOB*): Look, I'm not here to check if somebody's screwing a few extra pounds out of us. It's my other departmental hat I'm wearing tonight.

BOB: What hat?

VISITOR: Funny how nobody remembers we're not just the Department of Social Security – I hate that word Security, it's taken on so many unpleasant connotations – but we are also the Department of Health.

He sits by BOB.

BOB: Well, there's nought wrong with me.

VISITOR: It's not you I'm worried about.

BOB: Well, is she sick?

VISITOR: I wouldn't like to pass judgement. But there's not just her in the house. (*Patiently.*) There are children here, Mr Huddlestone.

BOB (*shrugs*): They're OK.

VISITOR: Are you sure? Confidentially, we have reason to be concerned for their welfare. If there's anything you can tell us might put our mind at rest?

BOB (*pause*): It's her you're after, not me, in't it? That's your game, in't it?

VISITOR (*gently*): It's never a game with children involved.

BOB (*giving in*): Ye', well, I don't see that a couple of bags of soil are ought to be worried about.

VISITOR: Do you have children yourself?

BOB: No.

VISITOR: I do. (*Pause.*) Have you noticed anything else out of the ordinary?

BOB: Well, I, there were . . . Look, I dunno. Once you started saying things everything gets out of proportion, dun't it?

VISITOR: There was what?

BOB: No, it's nought. It's just she's ever so particular 'bout not being disturbed after the kids are in bed. Said she went to bed early herself.

VISITOR: And does she?

BOB: Kids are very tiring, aren't they?

VISITOR: So she goes to bed early?

BOB: Well, no, not really. Not unless she's stone deaf.

VISITOR: How do you mean?

BOB: Well, she plays the stereo full blast for hours. And tonight when I came down, she were in her dressing-gown but the bed won't made up.

VISITOR (*pause*): Was she alone?

BOB: Oh, ye'.

VISITOR: She answered the door straight away?

BOB: Well, no, but I guess that's cause she din't hear me at first.

VISITOR: Unusual to have a lock on a living-room door, don't you think?

BOB: Well, I suppose —

VISITOR: So she had plenty of time to slip into her dressing-gown?

BOB: Ye'.

VISITOR: And plenty of time for somebody to sneak out of that window.

BOB (*amazed*): What?

VISITOR: You can't be sure she wasn't entertaining a man in here, then?

Silence.

BOB: Look, I don't think I want to get into any of this.

VISITOR: Could have been though, couldn't she?

BOB: No.

VISITOR: Why not?

BOB: Well she'd hardly be entertaining blokes covered from head to foot in mud.

VISITOR: What?

BOB: She was having a mud bath.

Silence.

VISITOR: She was having a mudbath on the living-room floor?

BOB: Ye'.

VISITOR: That doesn't strike you as a trifle bizarre?

BOB: Bizarre?

VISITOR: You reckon that's why she has these bags of soil. That they're really ten years supply of skin care.

BOB (*confused*): You don't use this sort of stuff for your complexion . . . do you?

VISITOR: Not normally, no, but you have to admit it's a remarkable coincidence.

BOB: Well, ye' I s'pose it is. But you'd have to be crazy to . . .

VISITOR: One of the things my job has taught me is the world's full of crazy people.

BOB: But she in't crazy.

VISITOR: No, but perhaps this bizarre mudbath was not for her. Perhaps it was for her guest.

BOB: What guest?

VISITOR (*pauses*): The Midlands Bank manager from Streatham.

Silence.

BOB: What the hell are you talking about?

VISITOR (*matter of fact*): Probably not him, of course. But his particular obsession got a lot of publicity. And the world's full of sick men who'll copy any famous perversion.

BOB: I'm not with you.

VISITOR: The luncheon vouchers brothel.

BOB: What?

VISITOR: She said anything about luncheon vouchers?

BOB: Look, I'm lucky to get breakfast with the kids, ne' mind —

VISITOR (*sadly*): The kids. Yes.

Silence. BOB *stares at the room. Eventually:*

BOB: Are you suggestin' she's running a . . . what, from here? From an ordinary terraced house? It dun't make sense.

VISITOR: That's what Cynthia Payne did, isn't it? Madame Cyn ran her bordello for the degraded fantasies of bank managers and bishops from just such an ordinary home. Payne. Interesting name for a woman who gained her satisfaction from men crawling on their knees through mud towards her leather boots.

BOB: You're pulling my leg aren't you?

VISITOR: Mrs Sinclair is hardly the the first woman on our books to try to supplement her income in this fashion. With two innocent kids in the house, that clearly becomes a cause for concern.

BOB: I can't . . . come on, look around. It's just a normal family living-room.

VISITOR: With beds, locks, bags of soil, and rock music to drown out the cries? What do you expect? Satin curtains and French maids? At the bottom end of the market knocking shops are all like this. Part timers taking in punters in between changing the nappies. I see them all the time.

He crosses back to his briefcase.

BOB: No, there's got to be another perfectly logical explanation.

VISITOR: Any suggestions?

Silence.

BOB: Why are you tellin' me all this?

VISITOR: Mr Huddlestone, when this particular mud begins to fly, it's goin' to stick on everybody in sight.

BOB: Look, I'm not planning to get involved. I woun't have ought to do with ought like that.

VISITOR: They say Mrs Sinclair is very attractive, is that correct?

BOB *clearly thinks she is.*

(*Mildly:*) We're all vulnerable when it comes to women, aren't we? And once in a swamp, it's sometimes very difficult to extricate oneself.

Silence.

Perhaps you might be wise to consider moving on a little earlier than you'd anticipated.

BOB *is clearly having great difficulties thinking all this through.*

Can I just bother you for a quick look at your rent book?

BOB: Sorry?

VISITOR: There's a query over the figure we have written down. (*Pause.*) Just a swift glance and I'll be on my way.

BOB (*still trapped in thought*): Ye', right.

He slowly goes out. The VISITOR *checks through* KATE*'s mail and then opens the small drawer. He takes out a small bundle of cheques, held together by a paperclip. He reaches into the back of a drawer, checking, and pulls out a small boxfile. He opens it and takes out a couple of letters. He groans and nods to himself.* BOB *enters the room, unseen by him.*

BOB: Are you all right?

The VISITOR, *blocking it from* BOB*'s sight, slides the drawer closed. He turns, holding the letters.*

VISITOR: A slight acidity of the stomach. Side product of too much orange juice.

He calmly puts the letters into his briefcase.

Well, I'll better be off to my next visit.

BOB *passes him the rentbook.*

Ah, yes, of course. Thank you.

He speedily checks it.

Fine. No problem. You realise that this conversation never took place, don't you?

BOB *nods.*

I'll see myself out.

He leaves BOB *staring at the room.* BOB *still clutches his rentbook as he stares at the underwear, and the sacks.*

The front door slams to. A knock on the door. BOB *does not hear it.* KATE *peers round, wearing a cheap, simple dress. Her hair is pulled back inside a headscarf. She switches on the tannoy.*

KATE (*quietly*): How was your meeting?

BOB: Excuse me, it's none of my business but I couldn't help noticing the plastic bags in your pram, and everywhere.

KATE *realises they are now exposed.*

KATE (*carefully*): Yes?

BOB: Only I just wondered what they were for?

KATE (*pauses*): They're just bags of common garden soil, same as you might find anywhere.

BOB: But in a pram?

KATE (*quickly*): They're easier to move in a pram. (*Changing the subject*): How was your meeting?

BOB (*insistent*): But what are they for?

KATE: Er . . . bedding. Was it successful?

BOB (*persistent*): When you say bedding, you mean you curl up and go to bed in them?

KATE (*grins*): Ye', that's why they're covered wi' the duvet.

She laughs. He does not. Silence. He still stares at them.

KATE (*with an air of desperation*): No, seriously, they're very good actually. Full of decaying goodness. The bedding plants just feed off them in their sleep through the winter. How was your meeting?

BOB: What bedding plants?

Panicking, she looks around.

KATE: These cacti.

She grabs an armful of the tiny cacti from the shelf. She crosses to the pram.

You see how small these are?

BOB: Yes.

KATE: Well, just stick 'em in this bag and lay them against the radiator and by the summer they'll be an enormous size.

He still watches her.
She uncertainly picks up the knife.

KATE: You just slash 'em and slot 'em in.

Half to avoid his uncomprehending stare, she begins to hack at the sacks, sticking in the cacti still in their pots, BOB *backs away nervously.*

BOB: Right, well, I'd better leave you to it, then.

KATE: *Don't go!* Tell me about your meeting.

BOB: Ah, right, yes, well, there was one little thing I ought to mention that came out of the meeting.

KATE: What?

BOB: I'm afraid it looks like I have to . . . er . . . move out. Move on. (*He attempts a smile.*) Mosey along, as they say.

KATE: Who says?

BOB: I don't know . . . it's er . . . It's what the Americans say, in't it?

KATE (*extremely agitated*): I knew it were the base, I knew it were the Yanks who were giving you your marching orders.

BOB: They're not. No, it's just the job means I have to move away.

KATE: But you've only just got here.

BOB: Change of plan. They happen in planning. It's one of the characteristics of the job.

KATE: But you've just got your electric blanket!

BOB: Oh, yes, I know, and thank you very much, but when the bugle calls, you have to —

KATE: I knew it had to do with the military.

BOB: Not at all.

KATE (*waving a cactus*): Is it sites for them missiles? That's what you're up to, in't it? Admit it.

BOB: Honestly, believe me, I don't have nought to do wi —

KATE (*clutching at a cactus*): Why? Why won't men tell the truth? Why must you always hide behind all this fucking secrecy?

She screams out in pain and stares at the cactus stuck to her hand. BOB moves automatically towards her as she staggers towards the divan.

BOB: Here, let me help you.

She shakes her head, almost in tears,

KATE: I hate these things. They were my husband's. I've tried to kill them. I water the buggers every day. They still won't die.

She sits, exhausted, clearly distressed. BOB attempts to reassure her.

BOB (*with difficulty*): Don't get upset. Please. Listen, I'm not with the army. I'm not with anybody. I'm not planning anything. There's nought to plan.

KATE: What?

BOB: I made all that up. I don't even have a job.

She looks up at him.

KATE: But your colleague?

BOB: From the DHSS.

Silence.

KATE: Why should I believe you?

BOB (*embarrassed*): Would I be clutching me rent book through a top level planning meeting?

Silence. KATE recovers a little.

KATE: But why all these lies?

BOB: I thought you woun't let me the room if I said I was on the dole.

KATE: I'd rather have that, than some sod connected wi' the base.

BOB: Had a bad time with some of the lads, have you?

KATE: Not exactly.

BOB: I'd've thought you'd have welcomed 'em wi' open arms.

KATE: Why?

BOB: Good for trade.

KATE (*confused*): Well, I suppose so, but I don't have to like them.

BOB (*quietly*): No, I don't suppose you do.

Silence.

KATE: Were you ever a planner?

BOB (*shakes his head*): Din't have the qualifications. But I were in at the beginning stage, wi' the building of the new towns. In at the foundations.

KATE: Doing what?

BOB: Drains.

KATE: Drains?

BOB: Digging drains. It's very important, you know, without good drainage systems that'd be the end of civilisation as we know it. I've never been ashamed to get me hands dirty working on drains.

KATE: I should think not.

Silence. BOB backs towards the door. KATE is deep in thought.

BOB: Well . . .

KATE: When you dig a drain?

BOB: Sorry?

KATE: Something I've allers been curious about. When you dig a hole in the ground and you come to a clay section, you know, it's quite distinct from the rest of —

BOB: Clay?

KATE: And it's sort of sweating.

BOB: Sweating?

KATE: Little drops like sweat all over it.

BOB: Yes?

KATE: What makes it do that?

BOB (*pauses*): Well, it could be any number of things. The water table might be very high.

KATE (*urgently*): But how would you stop it?

BOB: Tricky to say without actually seeing the situation.

KATE: Oh, there in't no situation. It's just hypothetical. A friend of mine once had a problem like that with a hole. Mind you, it wasn't a problem. It was a swimming pool.

Silence.

BOB: Well, if you'll excuse me.

KATE: Fascinating subject, though. Maybe we can continue it another time.

BOB: Well, yes, that would be very nice, but it's a bit unlikely.

KATE: Why?

BOB: Well, with me vacating the room, and everything.

KATE *looks up from picking the cactus needles out of her palm.*

KATE: Why you goin'? You don't have a job.

BOB: Ah, true, yes, but . . . I've always planned to travel. So . . .

KATE: Oh. (*Pause.*) You travel a lot then, do you?

BOB (*hesitates*): Yes.

KATE: Oh, God, you're so lucky. Have you ever been to Canada? That's where I'd love to take the kids.

BOB: Oh, it's lovely. Canada.

KATE: Did you fly there?

BOB: Sort of.

KATE: Was it expensive?

BOB: Not exactly.

KATE: Did you go to Quebec?

BOB: No, mainly just the forests, and the Rockies.

KATE: Are the people nice?

BOB: Oh, yes, very honest, very straight. They speak from the heart, you know, not with forked tongues.

KATE (*pauses*): Who do?

BOB: The Indians.

KATE: What, you stayed with the Indians?

BOB: Well, just for a weekend. (*He attempts a joke.*) There in't many B&B out there. It's not a populous area. (*Pauses.*) Why do you want to go there?

KATE: Oh, it must feel so free. Mind you, wi' me it's just a dream. My ex won't let me sell up so we can clear off. He wants to keep his eye on me and the kids.

BOB: Is that unreasonable?

KATE: What?

BOB: That he should worry about them, with the problems that a woman . . . you know . . . on her own . . .

KATE: Are you married?

BOB: No.

KATE: Bachelor free, eh?

BOB: There was somebody. A woman. But when we come to the sticky bit we din't . . . er . . . stick together.

KATE: Was that when you lost your job?

BOB: I din't make it easy for her. Not by a long chalk.

KATE: But she din't understand what you were going through?

BOB: 'Bout the size of it.

KATE: I understand.

She smiles at him, sympathetically.

BOB (*backing off*): Ye', well, you must hear a lot of those sort of stories in your line.

KATE: Sorry?

BOB: All those my wife don't understand me sagas, and you offering tea and sympathy, and . . . Well, don't get me wrong. I'm not one of them blokes who whine on like that. So don't think I'm in the market for a bit of . . . for any sort of solace over that. I'm not in the market for ought. I mean I'm not the sort of bloke you might know who's into soil, or dirt, you know. No. I mean, drainage was just a job to me, not someat I got into on a Saturday night, with a woman. I'm self-sufficient, you see. Don't need no tea, or sympathy. I don't need to pay for company, somebody to hold me hand, or anything. And if I was, I woun't have to pay for it, which I'm not anyway, so I won't. (*He laughs.*) So there we are. I just thought it important to get things straight. None of this talking with forked tongue. Personally, I wish you luck getting to Canada, and I for one will pass no judgement on what you have to do to raise the airfare. (*Moving to her.*) I'm delighted we've had this opportunity to clear the air, and we're all above board, and thank you very much. I've enjoyed being here. Your children are lovely. Please keep the month's rent and thank you.

He holds out his hand. Somewhat dazed, she offers hers. He shakes it firmly. She screams. Unfortunately, she had not completed picking out the needles.

Oh, God, sorry. I din't mean to cause you pain. 'Specially not at parting. That's the one thing I hate. I'll get some hot water. You need to bathe it, or it'll get septic with all the dirt.

KATE: Don't bother.

BOB: No bother.

He goes out. KATE, exhausted, is about to wipe her hand across her brow when she remembers the dirt. She stares out at the room. BOB returns, with a bowl of water.

I'm sorry about that. I'm really clumsy, physically. It's OK down a trench, but with delicate things . . . (*Pause.*) Being a planner would have been right up my street. That's all vision.

He puts down the bowl.

KATE (*stares around*): Look at this mess. I can never keep it clean.

BOB: Occupational hazard.

KATE (*sighs*): If I could just break out of here, but when you're broke, wi' two kids. . . . (*Pause.*) I've tried everything imaginable to make a couple of bob.

BOB: I can imagine.

He backs away. She begins to bathe her hand.

KATE: Even tried writin' one of those romances. You'd think it'd be dead easy knocking out one of them love stories, woun't you?

BOB: Well, ye', for a woman.

KATE: It's not. It's a real sweat if you can't believe in them men on white chargers carrying you off into the desert.

BOB: And you can't?

KATE: Look, I know when they ride out again, it in't just a box of Turkish Delight they leave you with.

Silence.

BOB: You should try doin' a sci-fi.

KATE: Is that what you read?

BOB: Ye'.

KATE: Not for me. Adam drives me barmy as it is with *Star Wars*. It haunts me. 'Specially that bit where Darth Veda's got the princess prisoner, and they're looking down on her home planet. And then, just to see the look on her face, he goes and blows it to smithereens.

She shudders. BOB is moved by her clear distress.

BOB (*tentatively*): Ye', well, that's the heavy side of it but don't you like all that journeying around different planets?

KATE: Oh, ye'. God, if only it were true. I'd be up and off this crazy planet like a shot.

BOB (*eagerly*): Well, you can. You can if you really want to.

KATE: Can what? (*Pause.*) What, get off the planet? How do I do that?

BOB *turns away, embarrassed.*

(*Amused:*) Do I go to the foot of our stairs and start thumbing?

BOB (*reluctant*): There's other ways of thinking about space travel.

KATE (*realising he's serious*): Like what?

BOB: Well, for example, there's er . . . well, theories about mind travel. The power of the mind over the space and time continuums.

KATE: My mind dun't have any power. Some mornings I can hardly dominate a tin of beans.

BOB: It dun't always have to be dominate. Dominate's a misuse of power. No, what you have to do is learn to free the mind from being trapped in the physical. Then it can travel independantly.

KATE: What?

BOB: It's what some folk call an out of body experience. Astral projection.

Silence.

KATE: Are you having me on?

BOB: Lots of intellectuals take the theory very seriously.

KATE (*sighs*): God, I'd gi' my right arm for someat like that.

BOB (*impressed by her desire*): Would you?

KATE: What, to be free of this body? I just feel it weighing me down. Ageing all around me.

BOB: You've kept it very well, all things considered.

She looks at him.

(*Embarrassed.*) Hughie Green had one.

KATE: What, an ageing body?

BOB: No, an accidental disalignment of his astral from his physical.

KATE: Did he really?

BOB (*nods):* In a car crash. He suddenly found himself hovering above the wreckage watching the ambulance men as they fought to drag his physical body out. Accidents like that happen to a lot of people, but the real secret is to be able to do it consciously, and then you can project yourself to wherever you want to go.

Silence.

KATE: And you've actually done this, have you? You've actually freed yourself from the earth?

He hesitates and then nods.

KATE (*quietly*): What happened? What was it like?

BOB (*pauses, impressed by her obvious interest*): I was lying on me bed, and did a technique thing and then next thing I knew I was floating just below the ceiling, wi' out having even got round to thinking where I wanted to go. And then I was easing me way through the roof like you weave your way through a path of high nettles. Just sort of shivering the building off me, and I was out, in the night air, and still rising, and wanting to. I was surprised how brave I was, 'cos there's a thin silver chord that stretches like elastic and if there's even a subconscious fear it just snaps you back into your body, like a safety belt. But I just kept rising into the blackness, thinking it should be freezing, but, of course, it wasn't. And all the lights on earth just faded smaller until they disappeared. I must have been, I don't know, hundreds of miles up. And then there was the earth opening to the first glow of dawn, revealing what lay behind her veil of darkness, the sun passes his hand across the golden skin of the land, the silver blue of the seas. There won't no haze, no cloud. The earth knew I was there, and turned her best face towards me. She hid nothing. And neither did I.

Silence.

And then out of the corner of my eye, I saw the twinkle of my silver thread pulling me slowly back.

KATE *watches him. He grins at her, somewhat embarrassed but not denying his experience.*

KATE (*clearly intrigued*): Sounds great. But . . . well, it in't real, is it? It's just a dream.

BOB: Real or not, lot of people's lives have been really changed by things like that.

Silence.

KATE (*pause*): And can anybody do this, or is it like being a medium?

BOB: It's just a matter of learning the technique.

KATE: That's what they said about sewing at school. I never got the hang of that.

BOB: But maybe you din't want to. The most important thing is having the desire.

KATE: Oh, I've got bags of desire to get out of here, and it certainly sounds a bloody sight cheaper than British Rail.

BOB (*offended*): It's not a joke, you know.

KATE: Who's joking? I'll give it a try. What have I got to lose?

BOB: I'll leave you a book on it.

KATE (*standing*): Coun't you just teach me how to do it?

BOB: Teach you?

KATE: Coun't you just take me through it now?

BOB: What, here?

KATE: Do you need any special gear?

BOB: No, no, I'm not into all that.

KATE (*stands*): I suppose I have to lie down?

BOB: What?

KATE: Is it better I'm on the bed, or on the floor?

BOB (*confused*): The bed . . . or the floor.

KATE: The floor's filthy with all that soil.

BOB: No, stay away from the soil.

KATE: Anyway, I find lying on the floor bad for me back.

BOB: Look, I'm not really supposed to do this.

KATE: Excuse me.

KATE *opens up the divan.*

KATE: Not that this thing is much more comfortable.

BOB (*desperately*): You see, I'm only a neophyte really. I've only just passed the first level, officially. Qualified for solo earth travel. I can't go straight off into the astral, or the fourth level of different planets.

KATE: I don't care. Just take me out of this room.

BOB: I shouldn't think anything would happen.

She switches off the main light.

KATE: Do I need special clothing?

BOB: No, no, there's no clothing. I mean, there's no special clothing. It's a sort of come as you are sort of thing. What you have on looks fine. You can breath in it, can you?

KATE: I think so.

BOB: Well, that's the main thing. Breathing. As long as you can breath.

KATE: Should I get in it or not?

BOB: Personal preference.

KATE: I'll get really hot underneath wi' all me clothes on.

BOB: The top. The top will be fine.

KATE: I'll lie on the duvet. Soften it up a bit.

She drags the duvet off the bags. BOB stares at them.

What do you do?

BOB: What?

KATE: Do you just talk me through it?

BOB: Ye, I can do that. Yes, certainly.

KATE (*lying down*): What do I do first?

BOB: Just close your eyes.

KATE: Do I have to fall asleep?

BOB: No, not at all.

KATE: Only I don't think I could do that with you there.

She stretches out. BOB loosens his tie.

BOB: Sure you can breath all right?

She loosens the top of her dress.

Ah, good . . . er . . . Now, I don't want to go very far, not the first time. We don't want to be shooting all over the waves, and . . . er . . . So, just think of a place you'd like to go, but don't make it too far away. Not Canada, but somewhere you'd want to go quite near, like as if it was an Awayday. (*He laughs nervously.*) Ye', right, so just picture it to yourself, and I'll get prepared.

He starts to lie on the floor.

KATE: You'll get mud on your suit.

BOB (*jumps up*): Well, I woun't want that, would I? That'd give me no pleasure at all.

Sh moves over a little to let him lie on the divan.

BOB: Thank you. Right. Now, can you feel the weight of your body pressing down on the bed?

KATE: Yes.

BOB: OK now, just relax. Deep breaths. Forget your body. Let gravity take it in his arms, her arms. Mother nature. Have you got a picture of somewhere you'd like to go?

She nods.

BOB: You can talk to me while we do this, 'cos we'll be flying together. Right. Do you know Peter Pan?

KATE: Yes.

BOB: Well that's really, esoterically speaking, the beginners' manual on projection. When they fly out the window. So just like in Wendy's house, I want you to concentrate on a window. It can be this window into the back garden. But you have to visualise it. Can you do that?

KATE: Just about.

BOB: Don't try to picture what's through it. It's just a blue sky outside, that's all.

KATE: Like in Playschool.

BOB: Exactly. Now I just want you to imagine yourself moving towards the window, to have a really good look at it. Can you do that? Can you see it closeup?

KATE (*pauses*): It keeps coming and going in waves. Then it's just black.

BOB: That's normal. Just keep coming back to it. Because that's the only way out, you see. How strongly do you want to get out of this place? Go on. Try it. Try going through the frame. You don't know how to do it, but who does? It's worth a try. Just let yourself —

KATE (*cries out*): I'm through!

BOB sits bolt upright, clearly shocked at the speed she's travelling.

(*Excited:*) Oh, what? How the hell did I — ? Ne' mind. Up up and away. (*Ecstatic.*) Oh, God. It's like . . . are you there?

BOB: I'm with you. You may not see me at all, but I'm there. I'm through. Don't worry.

KATE: I'm not. I'm not.

BOB: Just take it easy. Don't rush it. You see the clouds do you?

KATE: Ye'.

BOB: Just look. There's one cloud that's a bit different from all the rest.

KATE: Why, has it got a silver lining?

She laughs.

BOB: Who knows?

KATE (*gasps*): Oh, it has. It has got a silver lining. More like a belly, a belly of silver.

BOB: Fly right into it. Right inside it. So you can't see nothing but the white of the cloud.

KATE: Oh, God, yes.

She grips his thigh.

BOB: What, what is it?

KATE: I don't want to leave here. It's wonderful. It's like being massaged.

She moves with pleasure.

BOB: You have to come out sooner or later, Mrs Sinclair.

KATE: Kate.

BOB: Kate.

KATE: Is it Robert?

BOB: Robert, yes. Bob.

KATE: Pleased to meet you, Bob. (*She laughs.*) Oh, this cloud tickles.

BOB: You won't be in it for long. It's a special cloud. It speeds up the journey. (*Almost hysterical laugh.*) It's like the Concorde of the Astral Flight. Just keep looking around that cloud for a gap, a small fleck of blue.

KATE: There's just the white.

BOB: Keep looking.

KATE (*pauses*): Yes, I see it.

BOB: Now let yourself go, let yourself fall through the hole. Just fall out of the cloud and you'll float down.

KATE *gives a slight gasp.*

There you go. Don't worry about the landing. The earth'll cup you like a well caught ball.

She groans pleasurably and her body moves gently as she 'floats down'. From now on she seems to be talking from a great distance, as if on the very edge of sleep.

Safe landing?

KATE: Mmm.

BOB: Now just listen. What can you hear?

KATE (*surprised*): The sea!

BOB: What do you feel beneath you?

She runs her hand across the duvet. BOB watches it with fascination.

KATE: Sand! It's sand!

BOB: Is that where you wanted to be — at the seaside?

KATE: No, I . . . I thought I were going to the pictures.

BOB: The pictures?

KATE: Well, I thought if nothing much happened, at least I'd get to see a film. But, oh God, this is a sight better.

BOB: So go on. Have a good look around. What do you see?

KATE: Sand. So white. It's a desert island. There are coconut trees, at the foot of a cliff. (*Pause.*) There's something moving there, a horse, a white horse with a . . . it's got a horn. It's gone. No, I must have imagined it. (*Pause; she laughs.*) Oh, hello, hello, little chappie.

BOB (*nervous*): What is it?

KATE: There's a monkey. Chattering away.

BOB: What are you doing?

KATE: We're both walking along the beach. Oh!

Her body tenses.

BOB: What?

KATE: Footprints. They just start from nowhere in the middle of the beach.

BOB: Do you want to follow them?

KATE: I dunno. Where are you?

BOB: Oh, I'm with you.

KATE: Are you?

BOB: Perhaps I'm the monkey?

KATE (*certain*): No, you're not. (*She relaxes.*) But I know you're here somewhere. I can feel you.

BOB: Keep wi' the footprints.

KATE: They're heading for the sea. I'm standing on the edge of the beach. I don't have any shoes on.

She runs her hand lightly over her body.

KATE: I don't have any clothes on. My feet look very big. My arms, my legs are . . . hairy! What the . . .

BOB (*urgent*): What do you mean, are you a monkey? Look at yourself.

KATE: No, I'm a . . . (*Shocked.*) I'm a man! God!

BOB (*with an edge of panic*): Do you want to come back, do you want to come back, would you like to come back now?

KATE: NO! Not yet! Something's happenin', it's fantastic, something's happenin' to my body . . . I'm gettin' a . . . oh, what the . . . (*She groans.*)

BOB: What? What are you gettin'?

She shakes her head and curls up.

KATE: Oh, is this what it feels like? God, it's big. Christ. I'm pointin' straight out to sea, like a weather cock. Like I'm calling. Like I'm calling.

She shivers.

Look.

BOB: What is it? For crying out loud, what is it?

KATE: You can see her. I know you can see her.

BOB *lies back with his hands over his eyes.*

Look at her, look at her rising out the water. She's so beautiful. She's no face. Her face is hidden, like there's a silver cloud over it. It just shines. But she's . . . I know that face. Who is it? Where are you, Bob?

BOB (*sighs*): I'm here.

KATE: She lies in the sand. She's whiter than the sand. Her lips, nipples, vagina the only specks of colour on the beach. The monkey winds itself round our ankles like a snake, pulling us together. Her vagina's like a flower. I think, I won't prick it. Should I prick it? I've got to. (*Half laughing.*) It pricks me. The monkey thinks that's funny. I'm bleeding. But it dun't bother me. Why shouldn't I bleed in love. I see her body like I'm floating above her. She lies on a bed waiting for me. The glistening sweat of a silver cloud between us.

BOB (*having difficulty breathing*): You're coming, you're coming back to your —

KATE: I've got to. Got to. It aches so much. Got to join with her. Got to — fuck her.

She rolls over onto BOB *who screams and leaps off the divan, staggering around, until finally he manages to steady himself by holding onto the pram.*

BOB (*trembling*): What the fuck . . . oh, my . . .

He opens his eyes to find himself staring into the pram.
    KATE *too is thrown off the other side of the bed, and kneels by its side, desperately shaking herself back to normality. Both are fighting for breath.*

KATE (*eventually*): Is it always like this?

BOB: No. Never. No.

KATE: Is it because we did it together, do you think?

BOB (*still shaking*): Yes, no, I don't know. I don't think so. A lot's to do with . . . Very strange things can happen, of course, but . . . I think, the main problem, the central problem is, you see, you're very physically orientated, very body-centred. On the other hand, you went a very long way. But even then you see your body's very earthy, very to do with . . . basic things, and it just drags you down to . . . Sand. Soil. Feet. Feets of clay, maybe.

KATE: Well, I'm sweating like that clay wall, so you might be right.

BOB *reaches forward and touches the soil.*

BOB: Do you . . . no, it's none of my business.

KATE: What?

BOB: Well, do you, you don't know any bank managers?

KATE: Sorry?

BOB: Bank managers. Just an idle thought.

KATE: Well, yes, as a matter of fact I do.

BOB: Ah. Midlands?

KATE: I think he's Welsh.

BOB: No, I mean, Midlands Bank.

KATE: Trustees Saving.

BOB: No, it's not him then.

KATE: What you talkin' about?

BOB (*emphatically*): Look, you can't go on with spiritual things if you keep, you know, speaking with forked tongues?

KATE (*rising*): I'm not with you, Bob.

BOB: I know, I know about your . . . proclivities. I know about your . . . evening diversions. I know about the luncheon vouchers.

KATE: I'm strictly B and B . . .

BOB: Oh, ye', and what's that a code for?

KATE: Well, I'd rather you ate out for your evening meal.

BOB: Exactly. And why? Listen, you have a soul, right, and you soil that soul with all this . . . soil, this filth, right? So make a clean breast.

KATE: What?

BOB: Stop lying.

KATE: I wasn't lying. Least not deliberate. There was a couple of times, when I got on the beach, when I thought I was somehow makin' it up as we went along, but then –

BOB: I'm not talking about that. I'm talking about this. (*He points into the pram.*) I know about the soil. I know what you do at night, wi' your door locked. I know why you get covered in mud.

Silence.

KATE: How can you know? Nobody knows.

BOB: Bedding plants! You must think I'm daft.

Silence.

Did you really think you could keep it a secret?

KATE (*eventually*): I don't know. I had to try. I was desperate. You won't tell anybody, will you?

BOB: It's none of my business.

She sits, exhausted, on the edge of the divan.

KATE: I blew it when I asked about the sweaty clay, din't I? I was too eager. It was just you wi' your experience seemed like the answer to a maiden's prayer.

BOB (*warily*): My experience?

KATE: I don't suppose there'd be a chance you might consider – No, I don't want to take advantage of your good nature. Only –

BOB: Look, I don't have any money. 'Sides which —

KATE: Oh, I'd pay you.

BOB: What?

KATE: Well, in kind. Maybe we could come to some arrangement. A couple of evening meals or —

BOB: I don't think I could contemplate anything like that.

KATE: It woun't take you five minutes.

BOB: Woun't it?

KATE: And I woun't ask you to do ought.

BOB: What?

KATE: Just take a look, and tell me what you think.

BOB: Just look?

KATE: Tell me how I could make improvements. I can do it once I know what's desired. Please.

Silence.

BOB: I'm going to regret this.

KATE: You won't. I promise you.

BOB: All right.

KATE: That's really good of you.

BOB: That's quite all right.

She moves towards him. He turns away. She rolls back the carpet, opens the trapdoor, and takes out the miners outfit. She holds it out to him.

KATE: You'll need this on.

BOB (*backing away*): No way. Not if I'm just looking, I don't have to get dressed up and —

KATE: But it's really muddy down there. And to get to the clay wall you have to go down a side tunnel.

BOB *for the first time really takes in the nature of the trapdoor. He stares down the hole.*

KATE: There's a ladder.

BOB: Excuse me, but what is this?

KATE: That's the basement I'm digging out.

Silence.

BOB: Would you mind if I sat down for a sec?

KATE: No, not at all.

BOB: Thank you.

He sits, looking from the hole to the bags of soil to the miner's gear KATE holds out for him. It all takes him some time.

BOB: Mrs Sinclair.

KATE: Kate.

BOB: Kate. I don't know how to say this. (*Pause.*) I was joking about the luncheon vouchers.

KATE (*perplexed*): Oh, good.

He nods at her. She smiles.

BOB: Do you sweat, I mean is there a lot of sweating?

KATE: Not a lot, but if I'm goin' to store stuff down there.

BOB (*pause*): It's a bit of an odd place for a basement. In the middle of the front room.

KATE: Is it? I've never really thought about it.

She offers the miner's gear.

BOB (*stands*): Thank you.

He looks around for somewhere to change.

KATE: This is really most kind.

BOB: Not at all. What are you thinking of storing down there?

KATE: The usual, you know.

BOB: Oh, yes.

She turns her back on him as he begins to undress.

You must have dug out tons of soil.

KATE: Well, I work on it most nights. It's a sort of hobby.

BOB: Yes, I can see that. I can see how it could be.

KATE (*turning*): 'Course for you it's a profession really, in't it?

He stands in his underwear. She looks at him. He stops. Silence.

KATE (*eventually*): Pardon me.

She turns away. BOB puts on the suit.

BOB: Strange wearing this gear again.

KATE: It's me father's.

BOB: He gives you a hand, does he?

KATE: He's dead. He was a coalminer.

BOB (*indicating the hole*): Carrying on the family traditions are you?

KATE: I hope not. All he dug out the ground was chronic bronchitis.

Silence. He stands by the edge.

BOB: Right. Well, I'm about set. Is it a long way down? Will I need oxygen?

KATE: Just as long as you can swim.

BOB: I can't.

KATE: I was joking.

BOB (*smiles*): Oh, right.

He puts on the helmet, and begins his descent. She drags the anglepoise over as he disappears.

KATE: Is this better?

BOB (*from below*): Wha'?

She switches on the light. The sound of BOB falling, and a crash.

KATE: Oh, sorry.

BOB: S'all right.

KATE: I should have told you about them shovels.

BOB: No bones broke. Is it this far section?

KATE: Ye', what do you think?

BOB: A bit of first aid should do the trick. (*Pause.*) Fantastic. You really shifted all this yourself?

KATE (*kneeling*): The worse problem

was gettin' shut of it. First, I dumped it out the back and told the neighbours I was landscaping but it looked more like a ski slope. I lived in dread of an avalanche. So then I wheeled it out in the pram, to chuck it off the bridge at night, but a pensioner jumped in to save the baby. Fortunately the river was low. But the police are still looking for me. (*Pause.*) Now I dump it up the golf course. Every time I go up there, they lose a green. My husband's a member. It gi's me a lot of pleasure.

She lets her hair down for the first time.

BOB: Coming up for air, guv'nor.

BOB *surfaces. Silence, only broken by the sound of a child sighing in his sleep. He sits by her on the edge of the trap. BOB's attitude to KATE has clearly changed and it seems that he now sees her for the first time and likes what he sees.*

KATE (*nervous*): What is it?

BOB: You've changed.

KATE (*smiling*): So have you.

BOB: Ye', well this is more the real me. More than that suit and tie stuff.

KATE: I wish I could put on a uniform and say that.

Silence.

What do you think?

BOB: 'Bout what? Oh, ye'. No, it's not a problem. Looks to be a thin skin of clay. I could probably dig it out tonight.

KATE: I thought you were plannin' to pack and . . .

BOB: No rush is there?

KATE *shakes her head. Silence.*

KATE: So you think I might be all right?

BOB: I'm sure you are. (*Pause.*) That is, unless you want to move in down there. There'll always be the odd spot of damp, but it'll be OK for storage.

KATE: Well, I'm really keen to get it as near perfect as possible. What else would you recommend I do to —

BOB (*softly*): You do want to live down there, don't you? It in't a storage basement, is it?

She does not reply but her eyes never leave his face.

(*Gently:*) You've wood stacked, cut to size, perfect for bunk beds. Plastic water containers. A small sidetunnel for digging yourself out in case the house falls on the trapdoor. (*Pause.*) It's a shelter, in't it? It's a nuclear shelter for you and the kids. (*Pause.*) I see why you want to keep it secret. First sign of panic and the whole street'd be knocking your door down. You'd need a machine-gun to keep 'em out. (*Pause.*) You figure it's that likely, do you? Ye', of course you do. You may well be right.

KATE: I think it's best if you do move out.

BOB (*carefully*): I won't tell anybody. I don't have anybody to tell. 'Sides, I could lend you a hand wi' it.

She shakes her head.

BOB: Why not?

KATE (*softly*): What would you do, when all hell breaks loose? Offer to man the machine-gun?

BOB: Was that how your husband was?

KATE: Oh, he's all for security and more bombs.

BOB: Ye', well, we're not all like that.

KATE: I'm sorry. It makes me edgy just talking about it. Please, go and leave me be to burrow myself away.

BOB (*quietly*): I'd rather not do that.

KATE *studies his face. Silence.*

KATE (*softly*): Do you think it'll happen?

BOB *nods.*

BOB: They're mad enough.

KATE: Well, how can we stop 'em?

BOB: I don't know.

KATE: Do you believe in life after death?

BOB: Well, there's always hope in't there? I mean, there's mediums who claim to have talked to ghosts.

KATE: Ghosts? What'll happen to all them after the bomb? Wi' no one alive to haunt. There'll be mass unemployment on the other side, same as here. (*Pause.*) You talk about hope for when the body's dead, when my kids' bodies are dead. That's no good to me. I'll do anything to keep us alive. Anything. I don't understand life after death. Excuse me. I have some work to get on wi'. Got some letters I have to write.

She rises, switches off the anglepoise and puts it on the desk. He stands, uncertain behind her.

BOB: Should I make a start on the clay for you?

KATE (*with her back to him*): It'll be all right, thank you. I can manage on me own. I woun't want to be in anybody's debt.

Silence.

BOB: I'll leave you to get on with your letters.

KATE: Wait!

She turns to him.

KATE (*softly*): Don't go. I want your help. I don't know what I want. It's just I don't want to start believing in something that's crazy, if you follow me.

BOB: Yes.

KATE: I don't know what to think. I an't had a good time wi' men. They allers talk about how the leopard's going to change its spots, but I've never seen it.

Silence.

BOB: You have to gi' us a chance. Please.

Silence. She stares into the trap.

KATE: I like working down there. Keeps me from thinking. By the time I come up I'm so deadbeat I don't even dream.

BOB: You scared of dreaming?

KATE: Nightmares. 'Bout the kids. 'Bout their future. (*She shakes her head.*) I wake up covered wi' sweat. Trevor said not to worry. But it got so bad, I coun't face gettin' up, and I daren't close me eyes and drift off. (*Pause.*) All I wanted was to make love all the time. The fear'd just come over me, and I'd want to be at it like knives. Like it was the only cure. He said I was sexually obsessed. Said I was sick. Not fit to be a mother.

Silence.

BOB: I don't think you're sick, or anything.

KATE (*quietly*): Can you understand my reaction?

BOB *nods.*

BOB (*quietly*): Do you still feel like that?

She slowly closes the trap. She shivers and holds her arms around herself. He moves to her and gently touches her.

KATE (*softly*): Please go.

He shakes his head. She gently moves her hand to distance him slightly. They both just look at each other.

Oh, God. (*Pauses.*) This is crazy.

She moves past him to the door, as if to open it. She stops, then turns to him.

I ache. Do you feel the same?

He nods.

KATE: What do we do?

BOB *is also trembling. He makes a tentative move towards her. She reaches out and switches off the light. Sound of undressing.*

BOB: What is it? Where are you?

KATE: Bob. Can it be funny?

BOB: What?

KATE: I need to laugh almost as much as I need to make love.

BOB (*smiling*): Well, that part I can promise you. I don't know if I can remember the other bit, anyway.

KATE: It'll come back to you, like digging clay.

BOB (*nervous*): Aye, but I have to find pit face first, lass.

KATE: Tha mun look under duvet for that, lad.

BOB: Oh, right.

Sound as he bangs his shin on the edge of the divan.

KATE: Are you all right?

BOB: Nothing broken.

KATE: That's good.

Sound as he climbs into bed.

BOB: Oh, 'scuse me.

KATE: No, it's all right, please.

BOB *moans.*

Tha's at face now, lad.

BOB: Oh, ye', you're right. I can feel the clay. Sweat pouring off it.

KATE *murmurs appreciatively.*

Oh, Kate. Please, Kate. I want to see you. I can't work down pit wi' out a light. I want to see you.

He surfaces and switches on his helmet's lamp. KATE is caught in the light.

KATE (*laughing*): You cheat!

She dives further under the duvet.

BOB (*laughing*): Right, here we go. (*He sings.*)
Eh, oh, eh, oh, it's off to work we go,
we do our sums and get smacked bums,
eh, oh, eh, oh —

KATE: We'll have none of that, thank you very much.

BOB: Don't worry.

KATE: Bleedin' dwarves.

The joking and laughter subside but not the desperate physical activity, aspects of which are occasionally revealed for a split second in the beam of the light.

At one moment, the beam illuminates the ceiling as BOB lies on his back. As they change position, it reveals a figure standing in the doorway.

BOB: What the —

BOB sits up for a moment, and focusses on the door, but there is no one there.

KATE: Come on.

BOB: I could have sworn I . . . I thought I saw . . .

KATE: Seeing ghosts are you? Well, just tell your demon lover to fuck off for the night.

She pulls the duvet over them. When in the natural order of things BOB resurfaces, a MAN is picked out, standing by the table. BOB screams.

Sorry.

BOB: No, it's not you.

Focussing on the face, BOB realises the VISITOR is watching them.

BOB: It's you!

KATE: I said I was sorry.

BOB: No, not you, love. (*To the* MAN:) What the fuck do you think you're doing?

KATE: I thought you'd like it.

BOB: I do. (*To the* MAN:) Fuck off! Just fuck off, will you?

KATE: Make up your mind.

KATE surfaces. BOB turns the light on. She's dazzled by the light.

BOB: Listen, there's somebody else here.

KATE (*uncertain how to react: trying to joke*): Is there anybody out there?

BOB: I'm not joking.

KATE (*pauses*): You're frightening me.

BOB: There's a bloke here.

KATE: I don't like this game.

BOB: It in't no game. Look.

He turns the light on the VISITOR (TREVOR) *who smiles, pleasantly. He sits on the desk chair.* KATE *screams, and dives out of bed.* BOB *scrambles for his clothes having taken off his overalls.* TREVOR *suddenly switches on the anglepoise and illuminates him.*

TREVOR: Can I be of service?

BOB, embarrassed, retreats behind the divan.

Sorry.

He turns the light away.

BOB: What the bloody hell are you up to?

TREVOR: I'm terribly sorry, believe me, I'm so embarrassed. I had no idea. I did ring but you were obviously otherwise engaged. And just as I was walking away, the house in total darkness, I saw the beam of a torch light. You could conserve your battery now if you so desired.

BOB: What? Oh, ye'.

BOB turns it off.

TREVOR: And I thought intruders, burglars, perhaps even some pimply adolescent rifling through the lady's drawers. I felt honour bound. It would have been an act of moral cowardice to have walked away. I hadn't for one moment imagined — I doubt I could have imagined — what was, in fact, transpiring.

KATE *scrambles into the overalls.*

TREVOR *whips the light across to catch her.*

BOB: Take the light off the lady.

TREVOR: That's no lady, that's my wife. Oh, sorry. Forgive me. It did seem a cue for a terrible joke.

He moves the light off her.

BOB: We don't need any jokes, thank you.

TREVOR: No, I can well see that.

BOB: You'd better leave now. Anything you want to ask me should be done down the office. Not here.

BOB *attempts to get dressed.*

KATE: What would that bugger want to ask you?

TREVOR: Would you mind terribly switching off the 'heavy breathing' record?

She turns down the volume.

KATE: Fuck off, Trevor!

BOB: Trevor? He's not your husband, is he?

TREVOR: Didn't I say I was?

BOB: But he can't be. He works for the DHSS . . .

TREVOR: Oh, you told her you were on the dole? Been baring your soul as well as your socks, have you?

KATE: Was he your visitor tonight?

BOB: Ye'.

KATE: You fucker, Trevor.

TREVOR: What's a father supposed to do, Kate, when he hears of men queueing late at night, especially when he knows his wife's peculiar proclivities?

KATE: They were lodgers, Trevor. Prospective lodgers.

TREVOR: I admire the way you hand pick them. Most landladies just ask for the odd reference. Or have I misconstrued and wandered in during the medical examination?

KATE *switches the light on.* BOB *is now semi-dressed.* TREVOR *is in jeans, a loose jogging jumper, and a light sports coat.*

BOB: Listen, mate, I don't care who you are. If you're not out of here in ten seconds, I'm personally going to throw you out.

TREVOR: You're getting out of your depth, pal. You don't know what's going on here.

TREVOR *stands.*

KATE: Don't, Bob! He's a fitness fanatic. He'd like nought better than to break you in half.

TREVOR (*mildly*): The word fanatic I resent. Just because for some of us the body is a holy temple, instead of a whore house.

BOB (*frustrated*): You wait 'til I phone your department. It's got to be a breach of professional conduct at the very least.

KATE: Bob.

BOB: It's a bloody scandal. You people think you can just —

KATE: Bob, he don't work for the DHSS.

BOB: What? Well, who the hell does he work for?

TREVOR: The NHS. On occasion. Largely private work of late.

KATE: He's a dentist.

BOB: A dentist?!

TREVOR: I wasn't always a dentist. Once I was redundant, just like you. But I didn't lie in bed and wallow in my slough with Madam Cyn here.

KATE: You can say that again.

TREVOR: No, I saw that sacrifice and determination were the only way out of my particular despair.

BOB: How can he be a dentist! He knows everything about me.

KATE: Trevor specialises in being informed. He has secret meetings with other furry little rats, who grub around for what cheese is going. No doubt one of them works for the Department.

TREVOR: She's confusing you. We're not the Grand Order of Water Rats. That's for entertainers. You two might be eligible for that. We're merely a mild herd of benign Buffaloes.

KATE: Pathetic little gang of overgrown schoolboys dressed up in funny costumes.

TREVOR: I wouldn't dwell on funny costumes if I were you, Kate. (*To* BOB:) Kate has a somewhat jaundiced opinion of our Sacred Order. Hardly surprising as it upholds all those values of decency and veracity that she so clearly aspires to defile. Kate's always enjoyed throwing filth around. And I can see that in some quarters her mudbaths are going to be a very popular attraction.

KATE: What on earth is he talking about?

BOB *begins to laugh.*

BOB (*turns to* KATE): He's convinced you're setting up a brothel here.

Pause. KATE *grins.*

KATE: Trevor, it's all that bending down to shake hands with the backs of Buffaloe's knees. It's loosened your marbles.

TREVOR: You intend to deny it, do you?

BOB: She don't have to deny it. It's so crazy nobody but you would believe it.

TREVOR (*pauses: studies* BOB *with renewed interest*): Robert, I'm fascinated. What magic web has she woven over you to explain away all this soil and sexuality?

BOB: There's a perfectly rational explanation, wi'out gettin' into all them dirty fantasies you're trapped in.

KATE (*opens the door*): Get home to your new tart, Trevor. You can't cause any more trouble here.

TREVOR: Just one second, I'm talking to my friend here. Come on, Bob, if I'm the one entrapped, don't leave me in torment. Just free me and let me go in peace.

BOB *stands for a moment.*

BOB (*quietly*): Ye', why not?

He walks towards the trapdoor.

KATE (*panicking*): Where yo' goin'?

BOB: You're both just making this worse wi' all this secrecy.

KATE: Don't, Bob. I forbid you.

TREVOR: We're not children, Kate.

BOB: Neither of you are seeing this clearly.

He lifts the trapdoor. BOB *stands back, and* TREVOR *approaches, clearly astounded.*
     KATE *turns away and moves to sit with her back to them at the table.*

TREVOR: What on earth. . . .

BOB: That's where the soil comes from. She digs it out of there and dumps it up on the golf course.

TREVOR (*turning on* KATE): It was you who buried the eighteenth!

BOB: That's not important. Now do you see? It's just ordinary soil from a basement.

TREVOR (*reasonably*): But we don't have a basement.

KATE (*turning*): No, well we do now. So now you've seen it, sod off.

TREVOR: One second. Please. All this takes time to sink in.

BOB: There's nought to sink in. It's just a perfectly ordinary basement.

TREVOR: This is a perfectly ordinary basement? Fine. I just have one last niggling little question, and I hope you won't think it unreasonable, given it is a trifle odd to dig the black hole of Calcutta in your front room — what, in the same of all that's mighty, does she want with a fucking basement?

KATE *takes* BOB's *arm.*

KATE: Don't tell him. PLEASE!

BOB *remains silent.*

TREVOR: What, not another secret surely?

BOB (*lamely*): It's just a storage space, that's all.

TREVOR: Can't buy that, Bob. Kate's not the sort of woman who'd dig a hole in her living-room just to put up pickles for winter. No. It goes much deeper than that. (*Pause.*) Be interesting if I found beds down there, wouldn't it?

BOB *frowns and turns away.*

I'm obviously getting a little warmer.

He peers down inside.

KATE: You keep out of there!

TREVOR: Ah, this is why she picked you out of all the other blokes? Good drainage man. Very useful around the . . . er . . . what do you intend to call it? Dive? Basement bordello? Seraglio? Seraglio would look very refined done in poker work swinging, if you'll pardon the expression, swinging over the door.

BOB: Christ! Go on, tell him.

KATE: Don't make it any worse, Bob, please.

She turns away.

BOB (*sighs: to* TREVOR): Look, if you could just get all this filth out of your head for one minute —

TREVOR: This from a man who makes love to my wife, wearing a pit helmet and singing the Volga Boat song.

BOB: It won't the Volga Boat song.

TREVOR: What was it then?

BOB (*embarrassed*): It was the dwarves' song from *Snow White.*

TREVOR: Dwarves? Coal mining dwarves. It's positively Wagnerian. I must say there's no shortage of imagination here.

BOB: It's only yours that is running rampant here.

TREVOR: Rampant? (*Pause.*) Bob, I think you may be misinterpreting my motivation in all this. That you see me as some deranged husband, dreaming of the day he can seize his rightful kingdom back. Look, I walked out, not her. I could no longer tolerate her increasing obsession for the type of games that you indulge in, which seemed to me symptomatic of a lack of sensitivity more suitable to a whore than the mother of two golden children. I walked out, to find new love, based on respect. But I have not turned my back on my family. I've attempted to exert what restraining influence I could to safeguard the future of my children. It is blatantly clear they can hardly stay under her protection. And it is their future welfare that is my primary concern.

KATE *claps.*

KATE: Great speech, Trev. You're really good wi' words. Must come wi' looking at tongues and teeth all day. Now you've said your bit, just sod off back to your new fancy woman.

TREVOR: There is no fancy woman, Kate. After the divorce, there will be a new wife. And a new mother.

KATE: You're dreaming, Trev. They'll never give you the kids. No way.

TREVOR (*quietly*): Kate, can we speak privately? There's no need for what I have to say to be broadcast publicly.

KATE: We've had our last private little chat, Trevor. Fat load of good any of them ever did me.

TREVOR: Listen to me, love, I don't want to drag you through the courts, but I have enough evidence to convince even the most biased of judges, like starry eyes here, that you are no fit mother.

BOB: You coun't convince me of the time of day.

TREVOR (*hesitates: then*): All right. If that's the way you want it. Bob, do you wonder how she makes her money seeing how she's not got a fortune stashed away, and she'd hardly pay the milk bill with what you give her? Perhaps she's taken to a successful new career in literature. That's why she needs the new typewriter.

BOB: Well, she did try her hand at romances.

TREVOR: Romances? Is that what she calls them? And has she shown you any of the fruits of her creative endeavour?

BOB: No.

TREVOR (*turns to her*): Not like our Kate to be so modest.

KATE *crosses over to the table and checks the drawer.*

Oh, there she goes. Maybe going to read to us from her latest work in progress. How stimulating. (*Quietly.*) They're in the blue folder, my dear.

She turns.

KATE: You sneaky little bastard.

TREVOR: Come on, Kate. Just a little titbit for Robert here.

BOB *stares at her.*

Not in good voice, eh? Well, allow me.

He takes out the letters from his jacket pocket.

KATE: Give those to me.

TREVOR: Are you admitting they're yours, Snow White?

She turns away.

Romances? Certainly one might be tempted to call these love letters if it wasn't for the final suggestion on what

will occur when the two of them get together, and the PS about the enclosed cheque. Would you like to read her poetic reply?

KATE: All right, Trevor. Enough.

KATE *sits by the desk. He holds it out to* BOB.

BOB (*pause*): I don't read other people's letters.

BOB *turns away.* KATE *watches him.* BOB *very quietly, almost as though he was taking no interest in the proceedings, puts on his shoes and socks.*

TREVOR (*sadly*): Well, your boyfriend may not want to face reality, but I'm sure the judge will.

Silence. He puts the letters back inside his pocket.

KATE (*exhausted*): Have you finished?

TREVOR (*softly*): Did you really think you could hide all this from me, Kate? I *know* you. All this sex correspondence course, obscene records, kinky costumes, it was a road I saw you doomed to descend.

KATE: Well, it were your idea.

TREVOR: What?

KATE: Not like you to forget, Trevor. When I think of you, I always think of elephants. After I told you where to stick your money, you were positively graphic about the only possible position I could take to earn ought. And them magazines tucked away at the bottom of your fishing gear were a mine of information for the self-employed.

TREVOR: They were given me for the golfing tips.

KATE (*exhausted*): I couldn't care less. Go home, Trevor. You've done your worst. Leave me be.

TREVOR: Not yet, Kate. I still have to see the final depths to which you've sunk.

KATE: You don't want to go down there, Trev . . . You'll only get your nice new jacket filthy.

TREVOR: I must see it, Kate. I need that image of hell to steal me for the filth I'll have to wade through to save my children.

KATE: Well, I'd be delighted to take you on a guided tour, but I've got my first plastic sexware party in the kitchen in five minutes and I still haven't worked out how you get the batteries into the saucepan handles. Why don't you pop back tomorrow with your solicitor?

TREVOR: And the cupboard will be bare. No way.

KATE: You're right, of course. Please.

She stands by the side of the trapdoor.

Be careful of the inflatable security guard, she gets easily over-excited.

TREVOR *moves towards the trap.*

Careful with your clothes. I woun't want a Buffalo to shake hands with you and find a lump of shit.

He takes off his jacket. She offers him the helmet. He puts it on.

You'll need this, O light of my life.

He takes it and switches it on.

TREVOR (*quietly*): You realise you have lost the children?

She stands back. He descends. The sound of her young daughter SARAH whimpering. KATE moves back to turn up the speaker. SARAH is crying.

KATE: What kind of man can take his own sleeping kids for pornography?

She carries it to the trap, and turns it up full blast.

Here, someat to keep you amused.

She throws the speaker down, and slaps the trapdoor shut. Sound of a crash and yelling. She drags the pram over the hole, and dances triumphant, ecstatic.

I've got him! I've got the heffalump, Christopher Robin. Oh, God, it's great, having the devil trapped beneath your feet.

She stops and listens. Sound of banging and yelling, topped by the child's cry.

Can he breath down there?

BOB (*quietly*): There's air through the floorboards.

KATE: Shame. (*She stands.*) I'd better go and see to Sarah. (*She pauses.*) You must think you've walked into a madhouse.

BOB *remains silent. She goes out. He crosses to the trap and for a moment it seems he might push the pram aside. He clearly thinks better of it, and sits on the chair with TREVOR's coat on it. The noise from underground subsides. Eventually, carefully, he extricates the letters from TREVOR's inside pocket, and begins to read. KATE returns.*

Every time that bastard comes round, she has a nightmare.

She realises he is reading the letters. He puts them to one side. Silence.

I thought you din't read other folks letters.

Silence.

BOB: Are they all like this one?

Quietly, she takes the folder out and empties its content into the pram.

KATE: Here, read 'em for yourself. You like a good read, don't you?

BOB *stands and stares at them. He throws the other letters in with them.*

BOB (*with restraint*): Have they . . . ?

KATE: What? (*Pauses.*) Fucked me? Oh, yes, I can truly say I've been had by British Mail on a regular basis.

BOB: Stop it! I'm just trying to get at the truth here.

KATE *looks exhausted.*

KATE: They're just letters, Bob. They pay me to play out their fantasies by return of post.

Silence.

BOB (*insistent*): But you don't actually meet them, sleep with them?

KATE: What difference does it make?

BOB: It makes a hell of difference.

KATE: Why? I have to go through it all with them, in my head. I have to imagine it. What's the difference but distance?

Silence.

BOB (*struggling to repress his fury; almost inarticulate*): Would we have ended up in there, eh? What we did would that have become food for your sick imaginings?

KATE: I don't know, Bob. What did you have in mind?

For a moment it looks as though he might strike her. She does not move.

BOB: Right. Just remember, there was one bloke who din't use violence, who tried to understand, but you woun't let him in.

He moves to the door.

KATE: Bob, how else could I get the money for the shelter?

BOB (*turns: quietly*): Let me save you the sweat so you don't throw any more money down that drain. 'Cos that's what it is, a useless good for nothing drain. It an't got a snowball's chance in hell of helpin' you survive. If the house don't collapse and crush you, if somehow, God knows how, you solve the problem of filtering the contaminated air, you're still, sooner or later, goin' to have to crawl your way out of there. And when you do, it in't goin' to be like diggin' your way out of Stalag 13. There'll be no blue skies and freedom to run to. The lack of untouched water alone will kill you within a few days, and God knows what else'll have got you before then, but I'm only an expert in water supplies and drainage. (*Pause.*) Nothing in your worst nightmares, would be as grim as surviving for even them few days. Surviving longer is impossible. Your shelter's a fantasy. Leave it to the madmen, like him. Come the four minute warning, you'd do better takin' the kids be the hand and strolling out into the middle of the mainroad.

Silence.

KATE: But . . . you were goin' to help me build it. You knew all this and you . . . ?

He moves to the door.

(*Almost crying:*) You've no right, you've no right to say that.

BOB: I'm sorry, but it's the truth.

KATE: You liar!

BOB: I'm not. You know it's true. You've just been trying to kid yourself with all this.

KATE (*near to tears*): It's not true you're sorry. You loved tellin' me that. Twistin' the knife in.

BOB (*uncertain*): No, that's not right. I just —

KATE: Oh, ye', course, you're so different from these men, aren't you? You woun't harm a woman, would you? You're like our Trevor. Woun't lay a finger on a woman. No, your hands are clean, aren't they? *Why don't you listen to what you say?* There's always words, in't there? Trev always used words against me. Not that he can use words better than me. I can make up fairy tales and write letters men'll even pay to see. No, he's no better. Just different. He uses words like a man, like they're pint mugs smashed across the edge of a Glasgow bar, splinterin' them into razor edges to slash the flesh of me. What's the difference between that and muscle? (*Pause.*) And you, you're so different? One night and you feel you've the divine right to cut me up with the truth, and walk away in comfort. I have to pay you with my blood for a fuck. And you can sneer at me for asking only money for myself.

BOB (*disturbed*): Look, I just told you the truth. What you do wi' it is up to you.

KATE (*deeply distressed*): Admit it, you bastard, admit it, admit you felt joy at doing me down, joy even at the sight of the end of the world as long as it made me suffer.

Silence.

BOB: I coun't have got joy out of . . . how could anybody get joy out of the thought of destroyin' . . . joy? What from? From hurtin' you? I din't want to hurt you. I . . . Why should I . . . ?

He is clearly shaken. He steadies himself by holding onto the edge of the divan. Silence.

You're right. I wanted to blow your world up, so I could watch your face.

She watches him quietly.
He sits on the opposite side of the divan, and stares at the letters. He looks up at her.

I'm sorry.

KATE (*softly*): Not pleading mitigating circumstances? That you were possessed, or beside yourself with rage?

BOB: I were never more in control of meself.

KATE suddenly sighs. BOB looks up at her. She begins to gather the letters together.

KATE: Some of 'em make out they're upset about the punishment they're going to have to gi' me, but I've been a 'naughty gal' and it's the only way I'll learn me lesson. Or I have to chastise them to get shut of some demon that possesses them. It's the same game, really. (*Pause.*) I wish I could still see them as perverts, but

they're not. They're just normal blokes who get a thrill out of living in a violent world, as long as they can imagine they control it.

Silence.

BOB: And I'm no different, am I?

KATE: Well, at least, you admit it.

BOB: What difference does that make?

KATE (*shrugs*): Maybe it's a step in the right direction.

BOB: To where? It was you who said the leopard coun't change its spots.

KATE (*tired: half smiling*): Perhaps I were wrong. Perhaps it's only acne.

BOB: No, you were right.

Silence. BOB stands.

I'll go and pack.

KATE: Is this how it ended with your other gal?

She has clearly hit a chord, but BOB does not reply.

Ye', go on. Go. Leave me in peace to let Jack out of his box.

She stands on the trap.

BOB (*turning back*): Take your kids to some friends for the night.

KATE: What friends? They all spy for him.

BOB: There must be somebody. (*Pauses.*) Leave me to deal wi' him. It might have been just words before, but judgin' from the racket he was making, it could be real broken glass in his hand this go.

KATE: This is it, is it? This is all you've got to offer as your farewell gift? More violence dressed up as protection!

BOB: It's all I've got.

KATE: Well, I've had that, I've had that, I've fucking had that wrapped round flowers from you men all my fucking life! It's no present! It brings me no joy! I don't need you to defend me.

My need for you won't 'cos I was weak. Don't offer me your so-called strength, your muscle! *Get out!*

He goes.

She hides the letters in the toy-box and crosses to the stereo. She selects a record, and puts on the Everley Brothers. She puts down sheets of newspaper from the door towards the trap. She pulls the pram out of the way and opens it.

You can come out now, Trevor.

She seats herself in the semi-darkness by the table and aims the anglepoise at the hole.
Slowly TREVOR *surfaces, covered from head to foot in a thick layer of mud. He flounders, out of breath, in the light of the anglepoise, like a beached whale. Eventually, with what dignity he can muster, he sits up. The record finishes. When* TREVOR *speaks initially he has a little difficulty owing to a mouthful of mud.*

TREVOR: was that dedicated to me, Kate, eh? (*Pause.*) Cathy's clown. (*He nods.*) Very funny, Cathy. (*Pause.*) Do I get a chance to make a dedication?

He slowly hauls up the speaker on its line. He cradles it in his arms. The sound of his daughter gently sleeping.

TREVOR: Was that dedicated to me, This child who saved my life, God bless her. (*He attempts to wipe his eyes. Clearly distressed.*) Have you any idea what it was like down there? (*He takes off the helmet.*) This bloody thing went out straight away. Cheap foreign trash. (*He throws it down the hole.*) Pitch black. A cavity in the gaping mouth of Hell. And Sarah, my child, screaming. Her father locked away from helping her, not knowing if the witch mother would ever release him. I tried to dig my way out of a little tunnel, and then the whole world crashed down on me. I thought, this is it, Trevor, but even then, under a ton of earth as the soil clogged up my ears, I was still straining to hear my child. I fought, I clawed at the earth, I thought I must survive, for her. And somehow, it's a miracle really, somehow I dragged myself from under there. (*Pause.*) Not that you care. You'd have preferred me dead and buried. What kind of love do I call that for your children? Possessive, destructive, anti their own father?

He shakes his head. KATE *sits quietly.*

I knelt at the bottom of this ladder, trying to work out where such hatred could have sprung from. At first I thought it must be something I'd done. Being so close to death gives one the possibility of real self-appraisal. I asked myself, where have I failed you? But, try as I might, and I tried with all of my might, all I could find was what? That I had occasionally refused some of your more excessive sexual demands. When you came on me like a commie tank division, nothing seemed to stop you apart from my total retreat from the battlefield. Perhaps I should have stayed to fight, but I've always believed it wasn't conflict you needed, but under-standing. And treatment. Not that you can get them on the National Health any more than you can get a good root filling, but there I could help. (*Pause.*) I still want to help. I bear you no malice even though you've just tried to kill me. You're not in control, I appreciate that. Look, leave the kids with me for a bit. You know no one can help you until you choose to face reality, and step back into the light of day. You can do it, Kate. I have enormous faith in the capacity of human nature to make radical transformations. I've seen it when men become Buffaloes. And there's no reason why you —

KATE *turns her head listening attentively to some other sound.*

Are you listening to me, Kate?

She turns back to him.

KATE (*softly*): You still reckon I'm building a brothel?

TREVOR: Let's have no more lies.

KATE *nods.*

Good. Now, what are you going to do with this black cavity?

KATE: Fill it in?

TREVOR: Good.

KATE: Do you think I should use gold?

TREVOR: You see, you're even getting your old sense of humour back. And what about this . . . correspondence course?

KATE: Kaput. It only made matters worse.

TREVOR: Excellent. Kate, I don't regret what happened if my proximity to death has helped to bring you back to your senses.

He stands.

I know a nice place by the sea. It'll do you the power of good.

He carefully picks up his jacket.

KATE: No chance, Trev . . . I'm staying put. And so are the kids.

He stares at her.

TREVOR: Kate, don't force me to read out your shame in court.

She smiles at him. He checks his inside pocket.

(*Furious:*) Why you scheming little —

He makes a move towards her. KATE picks up the paper-knife from the table and turns on him.

KATE: Stay there! If one bit of your filth drops on my lovely clean floor I swear I'll do for you, bury you down there and no one will be any the wiser. You din't tell her ladyship where you were going, did you? I'll park your car in the redlight area, with some torn female attire from my private collection strewn all over the backseat, and leave the rest to folk's imagination. I tell you this, Trev, I bet the Buffaloes won't stampede to attend your remembrance service.

TREVOR *does not move off the paper.*

TREVOR: God, you're sick, Kate.

She takes the folder and holds it open over the trap.

KATE: I woun't like you to leave without some little victory to take with you. I know how dangerous that would be. You see, they've all gone, Trevor. Together with the lodger.

TREVOR: So he read them, did he?

KATE: Oh, yes. Your understanding of psychology is as good as ever.

TREVOR: Why did he take them with him?

KATE: Book at Bedtime?

TREVOR (*horrified*): He woun't think of publishing them, would he?

KATE: Quite the opposite. He's burning them on the 5th . . .

TREVOR: Why's he waiting until then?

KATE: The 5th tee, Trevor. That one that's enclosed by the charming little wood.

TREVOR: What have you got against that golf course?

KATE: Nothing. I'm very attracted to it.

TREVOR: He could start a fire. That's a National Trust area. It's so beautiful no one's even allowed to live there.

KATE: You might catch him, Trevor, if you run.

She laughs.

TREVOR: You won't make a fool out of me, Kate.

KATE: You're doing great without my help.

TREVOR: You're not right to look after children.

Keeping to the paper, he makes his slow journey towards the door.

I'll not forget you tried to kill me.

KATE (*quietly*): Trevor, it was me who set you free.

TREVOR: That may have been your big mistake.

He leaves. KATE closes the hall door behind her. She leans against it, rocking slightly. Then, crossing to the sideboard, she switches the 'intercom' system on. She sounds almost in tears.

KATE: You can come out now. He's gone.

Shaking, she crawls across the floor, gathering up the newspapers to throw them down the hole. BOB enters behind her, mistaking her laughter for despair.

BOB: What is it? Has he hurt you? What's he done?

He moves to hold her. She puts up a hand against him.

KATE: I'm all right. (*Laughing.*) Oh, you should have seen him. He's always had a lovely physique 'as our Trev, but tonight he looked just like Tarzan coming out the swamp. Wi' a full nappy.

She picks up the speaker TREVOR left by the trap.

BOB: He din't hurt you then?

KATE: No call for the cavalry. Not that you'd've heard it anyway, stuck up there in Adam's room.

BOB (*embarrassed*): How did you know I were there?

KATE: Woman's intuition. Can tell you an't got kids, thinking these things worked two way. That'd be a sure recipe for a nervous breakdown.

She places it back on the sideboard. For a moment, she leans on it, apparently exhausted.

BOB: So he was all right, was he?

KATE: Oh, ye'. Fine and dandy. I waved a knife at him and he strolled off to launch the missiles.

She returns to the trap, stares down it, and then begins to unload the bags down it.

BOB: Wha' you doin'?

KATE (*sharply*): Have a guess.

Silence.

BOB: Can I give you a hand?

KATE: I think I've had enough of dirty men for one night.

She dumps them back down the hole.

BOB: Ye', I can appreciate that.

She retrieves the letters.

KATE: And that includes you lot as well.

BOB: How'll you survive if you chuck them?

KATE: They're not helpin' me survive, are they? They just pay me to dig me own grave. Well, I've wised up to that. If them madmen start a nuclear war, no point fretting about the headstone. No, I'm not goin' to be one of their zombies any more. (*She throws them down the hole.*) I want to live.

BOB: So do I.

She stops and turns to him.

KATE: Shun't you be half-way to Canada by now?

BOB (*with effort*): That's just what I felt like doing, when I twigged I coun't hear ought up there. (*Pause.*) But I coun't move. I was so ashamed wi' meself . . . it were like I was turning meself into a lump of rock . . . I coun't breath. (*He grimaces.*) I thought I were going to die.

KATE: And did you?

BOB (*smiles*): No. Your lad saved me.

KATE: What was Adam up to?

BOB: Nothing. He were fast asleep. All I could hear was his breathing.

He stops and listens to it again.

(*Smiling:*) It's like the house is full of it, in't it?

Silence.

So calm. It just took my breath wi' it, like you take a panicky kid by the hand for a quiet walk. (*Pause: half-smiling.*) And I felt so clear I could have projected to the moon then and there. (*Pause.*) But I din't want to. I din't want to go travellin' on me own anymore. I wanted to stay here.

Silence.

KATE: What? (*Pause.*) After what you said and done? You're joking, aren't you?

Silence.

Gi' me one good reason.

Silence.

BOB (*quietly*): Maybe you're right. Maybe it's better if us blokes just leave you alone. Least that way we can't do you no more harm.

KATE: You don't believe that, do you?

He sits on the edge of the divan.

BOB (*shakes his head: with difficulty*): When Sally walked out on me, every time I closed me eyes I could see her face. I used to dream of what I'd do if I got me hands on her. Din't seem to be no harm in imagin' my revenge. When I got into my . . . correspondence course, I were told I could be doing it, actually travelling out to her, tormenting her, subconsciously.

KATE: What?

BOB: It's what they call psychic rape.

KATE: You could really get through to her?

BOB: To her subconscious, ye'. It in't make believe. You desire, imagine, and . . . you can do it.

KATE: You mean like when I was on that beach, making love to that woman who come out the water, in some way that was real?

BOB: Ye'.

KATE: And what I did to her was this psychic rape?

BOB: Oh, no. Because she wanted it. She clearly desired it as much as you, whoever she was.

KATE (*startled*): You think she really existed?

BOB: I don't know. I don't know any of this is true. I just know that when I closed me eyes in your lad's room, there were a face in front of me. Only this time it weren't Sally. It was yours. (*Pause.*) And I don't want that. I don't want to go through all that again. I want it to be different.

Silence.

KATE (*quietly*): So do I.

He looks up at her. Sudden noise over the speakers of ADAM *bursting into life for a laser beam battle, calling to Hans Solo for covering fire, making spacegun noises etc.* KATE *snaps into action.*

KATE: Christ! (*Switching control on speaker.*) Skywalker. Get back to base immediately! Go to sleep now, or I'll . . .

She stifles her rage. Sudden silence.

ADAM (*voice*): May the Force be with you.

KATE: It'll be with you, right up your bum, me lad, if I have to come up there.

Silence.

I'm scared stiff, Bob. I've already got Star Wars in me bedrooms, and now those loonies are really goin' to put 'em on the moon. Even you won't be able to escape soon. Why? Why do they do it?

BOB: They desire, they dream, then they make it.

KATE (*sharply*): Well coun't you all desire someat different?

He turns to her. Silence. She sits on the far side of the divan. She's trembling.

Touch of me obsession. (*Softly.*) Touch. Oh, God, if only I could just lie on me back and think of England like in the good old days. (*Pause.*) I can't escape wi' the faceless fuck now, either. I've had being an ostrich wi' her head in the sand. Too many buffaloes come up and bugger you. (*Smiling.*) If you close your eyes now you woun't see my face but the bum of a daft bird struggling to get her head free.

BOB (*grinning*): That I'll have to see.

He closes his eyes.

KATE: I'm not sure I want you lookin' at me in such a compromising position. Here, you're not going to be the buffalo, are you?

BOB *shivers and gives a gasp.* KATE *watches him fascinated.*

KATE (*nervous*): What is it, Bob? Is it me face you see?

(*Shaking his head:*) I can't see ought. It's like I'm looking through water. I can't breath.

KATE: Are you being serious?

BOB *begins to fight for his breath. He lies back. She moves to help him.*

This is just a joke, in't it? It's not real. Are you just trying to frighten me?

BOB *struggles to loosen his collar.*

(*Trying to help him.*) What is it? Is it some form of fit? Bob, do you want I should get a doctor?

BOB: No, no, please.

KATE: For Christ's sake, Bob, open your eyes.

BOB: Not yet. Not just yet. Someat important's happening.

KATE: What? Don't leave me out of it. What?

BOB: I can feel someat callin' me. Or I'm callin'. I don't know, but . . . I'm in water, like inside a whirlpool. Just make out . . . a shape above me, above the water. Looks a monster, some sort of . . .

KATE: Leave it alone, pal. Don't have ought to do wi' Moby Dick.

BOB: I can't help it. I'm sucked towards it. Can you see it?

Kneeling by his side she closes her eyes.

I'm frightened. Are you here? Where are you?

KATE (*quietly*): I am here.

BOB *gasps as though surfacing.*

You're all right, Bob. You're all right. (*Pause.*) You're on the sand now. Take your time. Look around. (*Pause; smiling.*) Can you see the monkey?

BOB: It's pullin' me towards the . . . It's not a monster. It was only the water made it . . . It's a man, but . . . I can't see his face, but . . .

KATE: It's like there's a cloud between us. Do you want to see his face?

BOB: Oh, God, yes. Oh, yes.

Silence.

KATE (*gently*): It's time we opened our eyes, Bob.

They look at each other. He reaches towards her face.

BOB: You're frightened.

KATE: Aren't you?

He nods.

BOB: We din't travel very far, did we?

KATE: A couple of feet. But it's a fucking long way.

Silence.

BOB: I want you.

KATE (*softly*): Desire. Imagine. Make.
(*Frowning.*) Can we make love now?

BOB: I don't know, Kate.

KATE: Neither do I.

Silence.

But we can't stay here for ever.

*She smiles. They embrace. Fade to
blackout.*

THE FENCE

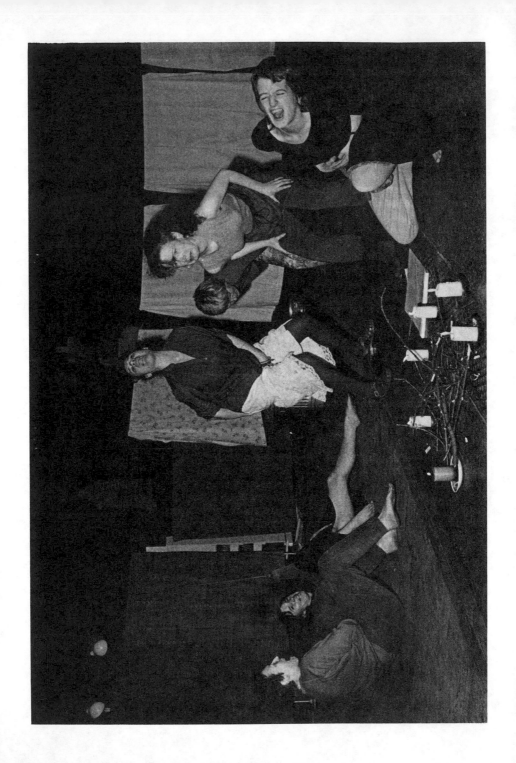

The Fence

I hope it's honest and unpretentious, and if it isn't, I'll keep trying. **Tracy Boden**

This play is based on trust. Half-way through its making I realised how depressed I would feel if we didn't get it together — it would be very hard for me to go on hoping for a peaceful world if we six women couldn't find a way to make a whole out of our very different paths. **Carmel Caddell**

This has been a journey working through fences, keeping going through differences, connecting with ourselves, the earth and, for me, the Goddess. She within me has given me power and strength to grow and accept the journey of the woman within me. **Max Holloway**

The Berlin Wall, Greenham Fence, moats, ditches, internal armories, all reflect the barriers we create for ourselves in our own times. Whether we cut, dig or magic away a fence, we are involved in meeting and transforming the *fear* that created it. **Tanya Myers**

Women together are strong. And together through this journey I have discovered strengths I never knew I had. Thank you women. **Fiona Wood**

I find it difficult to accept I'm a woman. Most of my life I've hated being a woman and hated other women, regarding them as competitors for attention from men. My journey towards discovering my power and accepting myself as a woman is painful. This show is part of that journey. **Sally Wood**

We'd like to thank: Ann and Anna, our wonderful and patient musicians; Sylvia for her photocopier; Janet, our lighting technician, for stepping in at the last moment and working wonders with not very much; John and Emma for the use of the church; Riverside Studios for rehearsal space; Simon Usher for faith and the dimmer board; Steve and Patrick for their lights; and last, but definitely not least, Greenham women for love and support.

Common Ground is a collective group of women, only two of whom had previous stage training, who decided to work for a theatrical expression of their common experiences of living and working at Greenham.

The Fence was built collectively and performed in London and at the Greenham fence itself in 1984 by:

Theresa (Tracy) Boden
Carmel Caddell
Max Holloway
Tanya Myers
Fiona Wood
Sally Wood

Production photographs: Ulrike Preuss

1. Isolation

The stage is dark. All the WOMEN *are on stage with props designed to elicit male-identified approval. Breathing and repetitive voices can be heard. One* WOMAN *is pacing and touching the parameters of the stage.*

TANYA: Why is it so difficult to wake up?

SALLY (*caressing pillar or wall*): Do you like my body, Dad?

MAX (*wearing a wig of blonde curls*): Feel the dark. It feels like velvet.

CARMEL (*in high heels*): One step at a time. I'm not afraid. I dare not be afraid.

FIONA *paces.*

TRACY (*crouched in a corner wearing a sash and crown*): I know there's nobody out there, so I'm talking to myself.

2. Male-identified women

A torch beam falls onto CARMEL *tottering in heels.* TANYA *lights a cigarette.* WOMEN *gather into the spot making sounds of self approval.*

CARMEL: So elegant, ooh so elegant.

FIONA (*smiling inanely*): Yes, yes, er, yes yes . . .

MAX (*through her curls*): Peepo peepo.

TRACY *pouts, emphasises her body outline.*

TANYA (*smoking, intellectually engaged*): Mmmm, mmmm. . . .

SALLY (*thrusting out her breasts*): I'm the best, the best . . .

3. Refusal

TANYA (*coughing, puts out the cigarette on a dustbin. Loud clang of lid*): No.

CARMEL (*throws her shoes into the dustbin*): I want my feet on the ground. (*Loud clang of lid.*) No.

MAX (*throws her wig into the bin*): I don't want this anymore. I don't need to hide behind my hair. (*Loud clang of lid*). No.

SALLY (*throws her bra into the bin*): Why are you laughing? Don't laugh at me. I won't be laughed at. (*Loud clang of lid.*) No.

TRACY *struggles with temptation for a chocolate bar. She rips off her sash and throws it into the dustbin. She eats the chocolate. Loud clang of lid.*

FIONA (*getting fainter*): Yes, yes, yes . . . (*She shouts into the dustbin.*) No. (*She runs across the space.*)

The WOMEN *are standing around the parameters of the stage with brooms in their hands.* TANYA, *visibly pregnant, is swinging a washing line now laden with six sheets she has put up during the refusals.*

Lullaby

I am waiting for your birth
Am I mother am I child?
Let you grow and grow wise
Lend us visions with your eyes
I am waiting for you child

Hoping that you will survive
The tricky demons and their games
They come in colours born of blindness
Come in colours born of pain
You'll need to look from deep within you
From your crystal newborn vision
And meet the many ogres, but
Not come under their possession.

I can wash and I can scrub
Your tiny feet your tiny hands
But will I make the time to clean out my
        sleeping mind
That may walk and trample your dreams?

Oh believe in surviving
Believe in yourself
Believe that your rising
Past the fences

Past the shelters
Past the bases
Past the powers
Past the half averted eyes
The half averted eyes
Averted eyes.

4. Sweeping space

MAX *walks into centre stage with a witch's broom. Silence. The ritual.*
She stands symmetrically with the broom upright.
Four pendulum swings with the broom sweep through the air to the north, south, west and the east.
Four pendulum swings.
Six pendulum circles and back to centre.
(*Repeat.*)

The other WOMEN *move into the space and start sweeping in various ways, their own bits of ground.*
Confusion arises over the boundaries of each woman's working area, leading to verbal confrontation.

Which Side Are You On?
Sung to each other in argument. Each verse overlaps to make chaos of the argument.

Are you on the side of silence?
Are you on the side that needs a fence?
Are you on the side that don't make
      sense?
Which side are you on?

Are you on the side that shuts its eyes?
Are you on the side that tricks with lies?
Are you on the side that wants me nice?
Which side are you on?

Are you on the side that likes to share?
Are you on the side that needs to care?
Are you on the side that's got trouble
      down there?
Which side are you on?

Are you on the side of the Earth Mother?
Or are you on the side of physical power?
Are you on the side of connecting the
      web?
Which side are you on?

Second verse sung facing downstage.

Which side are you on?
Which side are you on? Are you on the
      other side from us?
Which side are you on?

Are you on the side of suicide?
Are you on the side of homicide?
Are you on the side of genocide?
Which side are you on?

Third verse sung to the audience.

Are you on the side that shuts the door?
Are you on the side that bleeds the poor?
Are you on the side that supports the
      war?
Which side are you on?

Fourth chorus is sung to self.

Which side am I on?
Which side am I on?
Am I on the other side to you?
Which side am I on?

5. The fire
Greenham.
    The WOMEN *walk to their individual piles of sticks at the parameters of the stage. Candles are lit. Sound of breaking twigs. The* WOMEN *notice each other. A stick is thrown into the centre, followed by others, until all the twigs have been pooled. By candlelight they walk slowly towards the fire, picking up stray twigs along the way. They stop to look at the patterns they have created. Together they build the fire and sit quietly and watch. One* WOMAN *starts to hum a song, the other* WOMEN *joining in until the words of the song begin to emerge.*

Boundaries
You say this land is out of bounds
Our lives and our futures are out of our
      hands
This earth is not ours to put boundaries
      around
We'll grow and get stronger our voices
      resound

(*Repeated.*)

6. The media

Fast light changes to give photographic effect. Accompanied by pacy music.

1 MAX *holds kettle over fire.*
Caption: 'Polly puts the kettle on.'

2 WOMEN *hug and leer at each other.*
Caption: 'Lessies for peace.'

3 WOMEN *wave angry fists.*
Caption: 'Angry women harrass male visitors.'

4 WOMEN *claw at mud.*
Caption: 'Baby born in mud.'

5 WOMEN *are lying on their backs. Display of agony.*
Caption: 'Dysentery hits camp.'

6 MAX *flies over the back of two crouched women.*
Caption: 'Women go over the top.'

7 FIONA *stands with regal posture.*
Caption: 'Our inner cabinet leader.'

8 WOMEN *part the sheets.*
Caption: 'Snip, snip, snip . . .'

9 *Sheet is tossed aside to reveal* SALLY *standing to attention with a galvanised bucket on her head.*
Caption: 'Soldier is galvanised into action.'

10 WOMEN *run upstage and kneel with arms raised.*
Caption: 'Shoot us if you dare.'

The WOMEN *settle around the fire. The* SOLDIER, *with a bucket on his head, stands to attention behind the fence.*

SOLDIER: Haven't you got anything better to do than play around making fun of people?

TANYA: Are you cold?

SOLDIER: Yes, it's cold out here.

CARMEL: It's warm by the fire.

Pause.

TANYA: Do you believe in what you're doing?

SOLDIER: It's my job.

CARMEL: Is that enough?

SOLDIER: I have my orders.

FIONA: What do you think of us?

SOLDIER: I think you're mad sitting around camp fires making weird noises and singing . . . But it's a free country isn't it?

MAX: Is it?

SOLDIER: You couldn't do this in Russia?

TANYA: This isn't Russia. *This* is England, 1984. Are you frightened of the Russians?

SOLDIER: I don't want to be overrun by commies, telling me what to do, where to go.

FIONA: Better red than dead?

SOLDIER: It's not that simple.

MAX: But you make it complicated.

SOLIDER: That's right, blame it all on us.

TANYA: They've done a good job on you.

Pause.

SOLDIER: What do you mean? Think I haven't got my own mind?

TANYA: What do you fear, soldier?

Pause.

SOLDIER: I fear you, women. I fear your eyes. They trouble me, you're weird. You destroy the natural order of things. (*Pause.*) My wife doesn't look the way you look.

CARMEL: Does your wife live inside the base?

SOLDIER: No, she lives in Reading. She thinks you're mad.

CARMEL: Would she come and visit us?

SOLDIER: Over my dead body.

MAX: It's a free country!

SOLDIER: Free country's got nothing to do with my relationship with my wife.

MAX *is pacing angrily.*

MAX: Why are you talking to him? Why do you waste your energy?

Pause.

TANYA: Can you imagine a world without soldiers?

SOLDIER: Don't be ridiculous.

CARMEL: What would you do?

TANYA: Where would you go?

SOLDIER: It just wouldn't happen. There's been soldiers for hundreds and thousands of years. Talking about no soldiers. You're living in cuckoo land. (*Pause.*) Who else would defend you?

MAX *stands apart, watching.*

FIONA: And who else would keep us under control?

SOLDIER: It's not a matter of control. It's looking after people.

TANYA: I don't want you to look after me. I don't believe in the world you defend and you don't believe in the world I'm trying to create. So how do we meet?

SOLDIER: We don't.

8. Building the fence

In this section the sheets on the washing line are used to create a montage of images, each expressing a woman's inner fence, that which defends her from herself.

TANYA (*getting up she pulls the sheets across the gap that reveals the SOLDIER, as though shutting curtains*): I don't want to hear anymore. I don't want to see anymore. I'll think about it tomorrow. (*She walks to the end sheet and blindfolds and gags herself with the corners.*) I don't want to hear anymore, I don't want to see anymore. I'll think about it all tomorrow.

SALLY (*herself as the SOLDIER, paces up and down behind the row of sheets*): I'm a soldier, I will stay behind this fence. I'm a soldier I will stay behind this fence.

CARMEL *stands behind her sheet, then slowly walks forward with her left hand outstretched in appeal. The sheet stretches over her face and body enshrouding her. She stops.*

CARMEL: I feel safe when no one can see me, but I can't speak.

FIONA (*stands behind her sheet and lights up a cigarette*): Hazy . . . smokescreen . . . don't let it come clear, don't let it come clear.

TRACY (*walks along the row of sheets, touching each one in various places*): I must remember this, I must remember that. I must remember this, I must remember that. (*She reached for her own sheet, wrapping herself in it with her left hand reaching unsuccessfully for the line above.*) I'm not waving, I'm drowning. I'm not waving I'm drowning.

MAX *is standing upstage, facing the audience, and has been mouthing each woman's statements. All images continue simultaneously.*
   The SOLDIER *is pacing up and down.*

CARMEL: But I can't speak.

SALLY: I'm a soldier.

TANYA: I'll think about it tomorrow.

SALLY: I'm a soldier.

TRACY: I'm not waving, I'm drowning.

SALLY: I'm a soldier.

FIONA: Hazy, smokescreen.

SALLY: I'm a soldier.

Repeated.

MAX (*turns to the fence, shouts*): You're all hiding behind your bloody fences. (*Silence.*) It's no good.

She goes to the fence and pulls away the middle sheet, the WOMEN *retreat behind the remaining sheets.* MAX *moves to the fire with her sheet and sits down.* SALLY *takes the bucket off her head. Whispers, scurrying and titters can be heard from behind the fence.*

9. Facts and figures

With each accusation and question a screwed up piece of writing paper is thrown at MAX *from behind the fence.* MAX *shows little or no response.*

Do you really think you can change anything by looking into the flames?
pssst. . . .
What are you going to do about the Russians?
Psst. . . .
After a nuclear war, the living will envy the dead.
Pssst. . . .
Why do you think that deterrence has worked for so long?
Pssst. . . .
How are you going to stop wars?
Pssst. . . .
Think you're a heroine?
Pssst. . . .
There are three tons of explosive per person on earth. What are you going to do about that?
Psssst. . . .
What are you going to do about Maggie Thatcher?
Psst. . . .
My taxes are paying for you.
Psst. . . .
Why don't you get a job?
Pssst. . . .
What do you think about genocide?
Why don't you get a job?
Why don't you go home?
How are you going to stop nuclear waste?
Nazi war criminals were only doing their jobs.
On your broomstick.
What are you going to do about two-thirds of the world starving?

For the cost of trident the whole world could have pure water supplies.
How can you be positive about a world that can't grasp universal concepts?
What are you going to do about plutonium?
What's so good about lentils?

10. Visitors to the fire

Shuffling and giggling can still be heard from behind the fence. One by one different WOMEN *come and visit* MAX *by the fire.*

TANYA (*like a begging dog, tongue hanging, panting*): Give me the answers. I know you've got the answer. Please tell me all you know . . .

Jeering from behind the fence. TANYA *returns behind it.*

CARMEL (*a reporter with pad and pencil*): I'm from the local paper. Could you tell me why you're here? Excuse me . . . How do you keep warm at night? What do you eat for breakfast? Why . . .

Jeering from behind the fence. CARMEL *returns behind it.* SALLY *sits beside* MAX, *attempting to copy her every position, expression. Jeers from behind the fence lead her back.*

TRACY (*as a guilt-tripper with her head heavy in her hands*): I feel sooo guilty. You're sooo wonderful, I don't know what to do. (*Jeers take her back behind the fence.*)

FIONA (*with a large bundle of wood as a gift. Pats* MAX *on the back*): You're sooo wonderful.

All the WOMEN *are back behind the fence.* MAX *gets up and walks towards the fence. Sounds of uncomfortable shuffling.* MAX *pulls each sheet in turn off the fence to reveal each* WOMAN *standing nervously exposed.*

She hands each WOMAN *her respective sheet saying to each.*

MAX: Yours I think . . .

MAX picks up her own sheet and joins the line of nervous WOMEN *facing the audience. Gradually faces and bodies relax.*
Blackout.

11. Tribute to the Diggers

CARMEL: We want to pay tribute to the diggers who were a group of people in the seventeenth century who were forced by poverty and a desire to protect their community into reclaiming their rights to the Common Land.

The Diggers Ballad

Two WOMEN *are wearing sheets as aprons, picking up the pieces of paper left scattered across the stage. These are gathered up during the song and placed into the dustbin.*

In 1649, St Georges Hill,
A ragged band they called the Diggers
Came to show the people's will.
They defied the landlords,
They defied the laws
They were the dispossessed
Reclaiming what was theirs.

We come in peace they said
To dig and sow
We come to work the land in common
And to make the wasteland grow
This earth divided we will make whole
So it will be a common treasury for all.

The sin of property we do disdain
No man has any right to buy or sell
This earth for private gain.
By theft and murder they took the land
Now everywhere the walls spring up at
    their command.

They make their laws to chain us well
The clergy dazzle us with heaven
While they damn us into hell.

We will not worship the gods they serve,
The god of greed who feeds the rich
While poor folks starve.
We work, we eat together,
We need no swords
We will not bow to the master
Nor pay rent unto the lords.
We are free people though we are poor,
You Diggers all stand up for glory,
Stand up now.

From men of property the orders came
They sent the hired men, the troopers
To wipe out the Diggers claim.
Tear down their cottages,
Destroy their homes
They were dispersed
But still the vision lingers on.

Ye poor take courage
Ye rich take care.
This earth was made a common treasury
For everyone to share.
All things in common,
All peoples one.
We come in peace.
The orders came to cut them down.

12. In the court

The dustbin lid is turned upside down.
MAX *robed in sheet as a* MAGISTRATE, *a little deaf and sleepy.* TANYA *is gagged by a corner of her robe as the* PROSECUTION. FIONA *is blindfolded as a* CLERK OF THE COURT *to follow the proceedings. The three monkeys; See no evil, Hear no evil, Speak no evil.*
   Two defendants, SALLY *and* CARMEL, *in turn stand behind a sheet.*
   SALLY *is in the dock.*
   TRACY *is standing in the audience, blowing bubbles onto the stage and generally causing a disturbance.*

MAGISTRATE: I find the case proved against the defendant and I fine you £150 with £40 costs or 60 days imprisonment to take effect immediately.

SALLY: I'm not paying. This isn't justice. This is a farce.

MAGISTRATE: Take the prisoner away.

SALLY *is led away protesting.*

CLERK: Next please.

CARMEL *comes into the dock.*

CLERK: No 27, Carmel Caddell, defendant into the dock. Are you Carmel Caddell of 163 Holland Road London W6?

CARMEL: Yes.

CLERK: You are charged under section I CRIMINAL DAMAGE ACT 1971, that on Monday 17th of October at Portobello Green London W10, without lawful excuse you did cause damage to a wall of a building belonging to another person unknown, intending to damage such property or being reckless as to whether such property would be damaged. Sit down.

PROSECUTION (*muffled through gag*): . . . Spray cans . . . asked to stop . . . ran away . . . police . . . van . . . aerosols . . . me Lord . . .

CLERK: How do you plead? Guilty or not guilty?

CARMEL: Not guilty.

MAGISTRATE: Would you like to give your defence . . . or what have you . . . what time is it? right . . .

CARMEL: I am accused of CRIMINAL DAMAGE without lawful authority or excuse because I painted 'STOP CRUISE' on a wall. I am not guilty. I did have lawful excuse. The presence of cruise missiles in this country violates international laws against genocide which became British Law by Act of Parliament in 1969.

MAGISTRATE: Yes, yes, quite . . .

CARMEL (*continuing*): These laws forbid the indiscriminate mass killing of civilians; they forbid the use of weapons that cause unnecessary suffering and they forbid widespread, long term damage to the environment. Cruise missiles can do all this . . . and worse. All nuclear weapons are illegal.

They are a crime under British Law, International Law and their existence is a crime against humanity. These weapons are designed to kill millions of human beings, millions of living creatures, millions of plants . . .

MAGISTRATE: Will the defendant sit down?

CARMEL: Those who support such global terrorism are guilty. Not me. I am acting to prevent this atrocity. I ask you to uphold the Law of Life. I therefore respectfully plead that this court find me not guilty.

MAGISTRATE (*pause, thinks*): I find the case proved against the defendant, and I fine you £50 with £25 costs or 30 days imprisonment to take effect immediately.

CLERK: Do you wish time to pay?

CARMEL: Yes, 1 month.

MAGISTRATE: Yes, Yes, Yes . . .

CLERK: Next case please.

The WOMEN *move to the edges of the stage. Lights dim.*

13. The Newbury witch

TRACY *moves out from the audience, as though balancing on a fine wire. Arms outstretched towards the washing line downstage.*

TRACY: In 1643, a witch was taken by Parliamentary forces as she was sailing the River of Newbury on a small plank of wood, laughing. They put her against the wall and shot her. She caught the bullets between her teeth and spat them back laughing. They put a gun to her chest, the bullet bounced off her, narrowly missing a soldier. She laughed back. Then one soldier, who had heard it was the way to destroy a witch, cut her at the temples, as the blood ran she knew her power was fading. Finally she spoke.

She turns to face the audience, both arms now outstretched along the line.

By oppressing me you determine your own oppression. (*She moves along the washing line.*) How I oppress others and am oppressed only adds to the limits that we make ourselves live within. The limits of Racism, Classism, Intellectualism. And to me limit is just another way of spelling fence.

I am the woman with no name
You do not know my face
I am the woman with no self
I am a jumbled mess of all of you
I am the woman with no voice
Although I'm told I have the choice
I am the woman with no violence
Though I may destroy myself
I am the woman with no limits
And I'm trying to put the world right
In an afternoon between the cleaning and
    the washing up
But I will not be imprisoned by my guilt
And when I find myself there will be no
    fences.

14. Prison

TRACY *picks up a sheet and marches upstage. She pushes a sheet roughly into the arms of* SALLY *who has been waiting in the audience. The other* WOMEN *are lying asleep around the edges of the stage under sheets.* TRACY *pushes* SALLY *roughly into the prison dormitory.*

SALLY *stands lost amidst the sleeping* WOMEN.

FIONA (*sits up*): They used to burn us in the old days . . . the witch burnings. Now they encourage us to burn ourselves. All behind nice clean brick walls of course. Right in the middle of this city. Like Julie.

SALLY: Julie?

FIONA: She'd threatened to kill herself. Sometimes you'd go as far as that to see another human face, anything for attention. They'd sent her to the strips . . . no matches allowed there. Next day they put her back on the wing here, gave her matches and she

set her cell alight. We saw the smoke, the screws running down to the office to ask what to do. They can do nothing without orders. By the time they got back, she was dead of course.

Silence.

TANYA: Hello

SALLY: Hello

CARMEL: Hello

SALLY: Hello . . . They dragged me out of bed and brought me here at 2 o'clock in the morning.

FIONA (*irritably*): So we see.

SALLY: Where do I go?

CARMEL: This is your bunk.

SALLY: Thanks. (*She makes a big fuss over smoothing out her blanket.*) Are there any more blankets?

TANYA: No.

SALLY: Are you sure?

TANYA: No, there are no more blankets here.

SALLY (*much fuss around her blanket*): Well, I need another blanket. I want two blankets, I'm not a criminal like you lot.

FIONA: What's so special about you? You're another woman in prison.

SALLY: I want another blanket. I want another blanket. (*Getting more and more worked up.*)

OTHERS: Shut up!

SALLY (*goes to the door of the cell and calls*): I need another blanket. (*Waits. No reply.*) I want another blanket. (*Loudly.*)

She waits. No reply. She returns to her bed and looks at the sleeping WOMEN. *Pause. She eventually retreats under her one and only blanket. There is a long pause. Her voice and sobs can be heard. Eventually she finds her voice.*

SALLY: I'm a woman. (*Pause.*)
    I'm a woman. (*Pause.*)

Please come to me. Please . . . Come to me. (*She waits.*)

CARMEL *and* FIONA *go to her and comfort her.*

15. Finale

TANYA, TRACY *and* MAX *start a formation dance and song with great gusto.* SALLY, CARMEL *and* FIONA *join in on the second verse.*

It ain't just the web, it's the way that we
    spin it.
It ain't just the world, it's the women
    within it
It ain't just the struggle, it's the way that
    we win it,
That's what gets us by.

It ain't just the care, it's the love and
    affection
It ain't just the way, it's the sense of
    direction
It ain't that we're good, we're just bloody
    perfection
That's what gets us by.

    Chorus line is repeated.

Reflections

The group feels it necessary to include reflections on the working process, in order to give the reader an insight into the way our journey brought us to the point where we felt the need to share our growth. *The Fence* is not a text that can be picked up and repeated. However, we did discover a working structure fraught with both negative and positive experiences that, after seven months' workshopping, we would like to share.

Common Ground

Tanya Myers

I was seven months pregnant when we performed *The Fence*. Most of my pregnancy was involved with the workshop. The two processes became synonymous. For me the project was a way of integrating myself politically and theatrically. Like Tracy, I am training in theatre language. However, most of the group had had no previous theatrical training. The journey was not an easy one. Our connections with Greenham were what brought us together, and we knew we wanted to share, explore and communicate our questions, desires and discoveries. Often it felt like swimming in waters of unknown depths, unsure in which direction our horizons lay.

Throughout the rehearsal period we all participated in various protest actions both at the camp and in the city. For me our rehearsal space was never confined between four walls and a clean floor, though we had to work pretty hard to find this resource! On the 29th October we cut and saw the fence fall at Greenham. In November we swept the streets around Grosvenor Square, ritualising an exorcism of past violent events. Later in that month we keened across Westminster Bridge taking footsteps slow enough to puzzle many police but not illegal enough to constitute obstruction! Three of us were arrested in the House of Commons for keening; a spontaneous expression of horror in response to Hestletine's speech in defence of both cruise missiles and the use of firearms in the event of a threat to national security. We all knew what this could mean. The media projected an image of heroic self-sacrifice. For instance one daily newspaper had as its emotive headline 'Shoot us if you dare'. I for one had no intention of wasting myself or my energy by reacting further to their fearful reality. I wanted to discover our strength and a vision that would move us beyond what we already knew.

Throughout, we argued, laughed, disagreed and compromised. We cared for each other. At the start I had been searching for sameness; hence the name Common Ground. However the piece for me became the realisation, and eventually a celebration of our differences. Though it was never intellectually devised each of us emerged with her own voice in the piece. My lullaby, written in the lighting box at Riverside Studios, took me to the fence at Greenham where I was forced to confront my daughter's imminent birth with this cold war, patriarchal reality.

I was accustomed to working either as an actress, a director or a writer (dab hand at all trades); I found it difficult to let go of my desire to control the shaping of images. But, we knew we wanted to work collectively and that would mean finding alternatives to the structures we knew. Early on in the work we agreed to create seven roles which we would alternate and take responsibility for. These were:

1. OUTSIDE EYE (the director)
2. THE SEEKER OF TRUTH (the challenger)
3. THE STARTER/INITIATOR (the devisor of improvisations and motivator)
4. FOCUS KEEPER
5. PEACE MAKER (the facilitator)

6. REALITY CHECKPOINT (to keep communication with audience in view)
7. MORALE BOOSTER (for the days we needed encouragement and inspiration)

Decisions seemed to take forever and involved much painful and emotional upheaval. However the group helped me work through my resistance to collective play and the audience response revealed the wealth of such a process.

Who did we want to share our work with? I feel we avoided asking ourselves this question until the very end. It's all very well me saying I want to create positive, non-male-identified images of myself. But in lifting the veil I discovered strengths and weaknesses that made me vulnerable. Do I want to share this vulnerability with men at this time? The audience at St Paul's Church in Hammersmith were both men and women. The audience at Greenham was also mixed, except this time the men stood behind the fence with guns. The women sat scattered around us. Under the trees amidst the sounds in the woods it was no longer possible to discern where the stage began or finished. I felt all my strength and weakness at once that day.

The Fence. It exists. The miles of barbed wire exist. The guns exist. Through improvisation, we each confronted, identified with and shared responsibility for the fence. By subtle shifts (and some not so subtle) we edged each other through the gaps and nearer to personal truths. Somehow it was easier to perceive the fence as something 'Out There'. We became the fence, the soldiers and our own defence mechanisms, and we saw the personal/political dynamics of our lives gradually transform. As an actress I discovered and articulated parts of myself I had never acknowledged to exist. This was a healing experience.

We did not perform together after these two performances. Now we are all leading very different lives. I have a daughter of six months, and my life has opened up into another dimension. Now I struggle day to day to find the time to work for myself. I look to other mothers to share my joys and frustrations. As a woman, whatever the circumstances I am compelled to redefine my identity. I love the theatre. It is my language. Except for Tracy, none of us were professionals. We were a group of women searching for a truthful representation of ourselves. If the space is not given we have to take it. This is the theatre I want to see and the voices I want to hear.

Sally Wood

I am a 30 year-old white middle-class woman who abandoned my potential career as a school teacher five years ago, went to live in a rural commune and have since spent a lot of my time active in anti-nuclear politics. My only acting experience was a piece of theatre four years before. By June 1983 I was involved with the West London Greenham group and was visiting Greenham regularly. One of the women in the group — Tracy — talked about getting a show together and I knew I wanted to be involved. At that stage I had visions of a very professional show with many powerful women, and me being lucky if I·was part of the wardrobe department! The show was first mentioned in July. In October we had our first meeting — 12 women at Tracy's flat. I felt totally inadequate and inexperienced. Seven of the women had lived at the camp and I had always been just a visitor. I could hardly open my mouth. I felt confused and excited. When we talked about what images should be in the show, I could only think of 'camp fire' which everyone else thought of too. I was glad I was sitting next to Carmel who I knew vaguely from the West London group, and who I knew hadn't lived at Greenham either, though she had been much more involved than me. I felt intimidated because of inexperience, and because nearly everyone else seemed to know everyone else very well. I felt guilty for being a woman who chose to live with a man in the presence of lesbians.

We arranged to meet again about ten days later at Rotherhithe theatre workshop — an annexe of Dartington College where Tanya and Zouffi had been students. I arrived on time, about an hour before everyone else (an event which became quite typical) but was happy to talk to the students there and knit my rainbow leg warmers. This acting business made me nervous and I wanted to put it off. I was about to go home when everyone turned up. We had our workshop which seemed very structureless. At the end we did an hilarious thing — comparing our feet and bodies, and I was glad I was dragged in and wasn't allowed to leave myself out.

Because of various double bookings, and mess-ups, the next 'workshop' was in Tracy's flat. Most of the women were late, some came and then went shopping in Portobello Road, some women had been to one workshop, some to both, and some to neither. We decided that it was impossible to go on in this chaotic state — that we would never get anything done. So we decided to close the group i.e. accept no new women at least until the women who were already involved had organised some kind of structure to work within.

So we formed a group — Tanya, Tracy, Max, me, Carmel, Zouffi and Fiona — agreed to meet at certain times or certain days and agreed that at those times our 'theatre' group should take priority. This proved extremely difficult to stick to, as we all had commitments outside the group.

There was a lot of lateness or excuses for not coming. My own attitude was to try to work with whoever was there, but I often found myself thinking 'It would be different if so and so were here'. During the third workshop it became obvious there was a power struggle between Zouffi and Tanya. I suppose there were power-struggles all the time, but this was the first one to become obvious. After this we decided that each woman should run workshops or parts of workshops so that we didn't rely solely on the skills of Tanya, Tracy and Zouffi — the women with acting experience. The other four of us had little or no acting experience, but more skills in different areas.

We found a 'home' in Wapping, and did more workshops, but still hadn't done any of what I would call acting, until Zouffi suggested that we each had five minutes in which to act out in any way how we felt about the last week. For three of us it was the first thing like that we'd ever done, but we all did something. Fiona spent most of her time hiding behind pillars and was hilarious. A couple of days later, Tanya brought in the 'Diggers' song and we learned that. Then we did an improvisation around being a fence, and discovered it was much easier having a fence than not.

It had taken two months to get this far and I gave up hope of getting anything together. Zouffi was so pregnant she could hardly do anything and we all kept arguing. I bumbled through day after day, enjoying the contact with women but feeling confused about all the carry-ons. I actually left the group at that point and went away for Christmas. I expected that when I came back, the whole project would have been abandoned. I was despondent.

After Christmas, I rang Tanya and found that far from the project being abandoned, Tanya, Tracy and Fiona had worked over Christmas producing a structure from which we could work and that I was welcome back. Zouffi had by this time left for France.

At last *work* started. I actually had some idea of what we were doing. We also moved to Riverside Studios in Hammersmith which was much more convenient for most of us and was at last a permanent home. I rejoined the group on January 3rd and the performance date was February 6th. We worked three or four days a week, Wednesday to Friday and sometimes Saturday. We usually spent Wednesday morning catching up on each others' news, and got down to work on Wednesday afternoon.

We worked painstakingly through the structure. We spent a lot of time working on the first two thirds of the piece, constantly changing and improving it. For two weeks, Tracy was absent. I felt frustrated by this, because it felt like there was someone missing whose contribution had to be taken into account. We were always saying 'We'll get on with such and such and Tracy will have to fit in when she comes.' We could never finish a section properly.

We didn't have much time to work on the last part of the show. Tracy wrote her witch's speech by herself and worked on it alone with Tanya. Neither did we have much time to work on the 'prison scene' — the scene where I felt least comfortable because I had never been in prison.

I was very nervous during our actual performance in St Paul's Church, Hammersmith, and felt I was wooden. I was terrified during my first solo piece as part of the 'beauty parade' showing off my bra. No one laughed as I'd hoped they would, and I was swirling my bra around to a completely quiet, unresponsive audience. That was a moment of complete terror and blackness and I pretty quickly ran to the dustbin to discard my bra.

I had time to relax and breath, though, when we were sitting quietly in the centre of the stage with the only light that of our candles and the lights outside shining through the stained glass windows. I felt that was a time of true beauty and I started to cry with relief at having time to relax. I loved singing 'You say this land is out of bounds'. It was a beautiful centre-piece to the performance.

I was never happy with the ending of the show and I now realise that was the reason I was so nervous at the beginning. I felt we hadn't worked enough on it, and I had a lot to do in the 'Prison scene'. During a workshop I had broken down and called for the other women to come to me. That had been real, but I don't think it 'came off' on the night. I couldn't feel the need for the other women and I couldn't act it either. I think I needed to work more on feeling my need for other women, for me to show it successfully in performance.

Mostly, I feel positive about the show. We created something that was very beautiful, our singing was beautiful, the two musicians were superb and the lighting people were brilliant. We had an audience of about 80 people, mainly women, and we had facilities to make tea and coffee afterwards. I'd have been pleased to go to a night like that myself.

Doing the show helped me to change and grow, though not as fast as I would have hoped. I had the idea that if I could have the guts and talent to perform in front of a large group of people then I would be a completely amazing human being and all my problems would be solved, that I'd get on brilliantly with women, have a superb sexual relationship with my lover and be able to perform anything, any time, any place. The reality hasn't actually been like that and until recently my negativity outweighed my positivity about my ability to perform. Doing the show helped me a great deal in my relationships with other women. It's difficult to remember the traumas I went through feeling different and left out. I relate pretty well to other women now and better than I used to with men, and I'm glad I did the show.

Max Holloway
I am Max, training therapist, astrologer and mother of two children. This is my reflection on our journey to the production of *The Fence*.

Working collectively with trained actresses and amateurs caused ripples right from the start of our work. The amateurs viewed the project as a growth venture with the excitement of 'doing a show'. This went with a fear of performing and a wish for the others — Tracy, Tanya and Zouffi — to show the way. It took two months for us to find a structure we could work within, and know and trust each other enough to feel relatively at ease showing ourselves in improvisations.

It was difficult for us to confront and challenge each other simply and straightforwardly. Often we let things we didn't like pass unmentioned. As the pressure built up during the last month we confronted each other much more — interestingly, when we had the least time to spare. I feel I had a lot to do with starting the confrontations — as a therapist I have learned it's always worth the risk of taking the plunge and being truthful. It's very painful and it releases pent-up energy and usually ends with a warm honesty flowing, if not a greater understanding of the value of what each of us have to say.

There was a lot of energy in our group for the bulk of the working. As six women together we were saying how we felt about boundaries. When we stopped looking at the boundaries of the group and started to acknowledge our own individual defences, the huge differences in perceptions, lifestyles, politics and sexuality began to emerge. We learnt that in finding a deeper connection to our inner emotional selves and our own power by risking deep differences of opinion, we do not lose our common links as women.

The improvisations on confronting our fences were, for me, the most powerful. They show how we can cope when we feel attacked or oppressed. The section 'Building the Fence' is made up of images of pleas for help. Some pleas are more obvious than others. Tracy drowns in her own defences while people are only aware of her waving; Carmel has to hide to show her plea; I camouflage mine with aggression, blame and strip down my fence and alienate myself; Tanya pretends it's not happening; Fiona hides behind her smoke screen; and Sally hides in her soldier's persona. For each of us it was painful to admit our own realities. So much of this scene, I feel, is a vision of our unconscious, the us we fear, the us we do not want to identify with, so much of the bulk of our energy is tied up in this protective defence system.

On reflection I'd like that say that our way of working was very powerful. But a few words of warning. You need at least four to five months to work together and for each person to have a commitment to the group. This is a very sensitive way of working and growing and it should be seriously acknowledged that collective work means exactly that. Collective therefore means supportive together, whilst each retaining one's own powerful individuality. These are the ingredients for trust. Be prepared for extreme swings of energy and trust. This is essential to growth.

Theresa Boden (Tracy)

The Fence was an important political and theatrical threshold for me to step over. My politics and how I practise them have grown in importance, as they have in awareness, in my life over the past few years. Theatre is my work but unlike most work, when I become involved in a project, and particularly one in which I am an initiator, it becomes my major priority and discipline in my life. *The Fence* was my life for eight months. My politics must feed into my work, the two are for me inseparable. Working with women means working collectively, and this was an occasion when I felt I could use what I had learnt and received from Greenham to feed energy back into that source. Therefore my response to Greenham is in respect of my political growth. By the nature of my work I am at my best when being a conductor of others' emotions, a narrator of others' actions and motives, an empathiser. To be an illuminator of my own identity and perceptions was to lay myself bare to what I feared most, my fence, that I would not be able to make sense of all the people, images, and opinions inside of me. That I had no voice.

The piece for me became more and more about what we weren't saying and tackling — race, class and language. In struggling to find my voice and a way of expressing myself, I lost my language and reason. I found intellectual discussion unintelligible. It was like if you look at a word or say a word for long enough it becomes totally meaningless. That's what language and reality became for me. I needed to start again, get back to basics, to where I had come from. My panic grew until I had to take myself away from the group for a week to gain my sanity. I was even frightened of facing them with the black hole that was me.

I didn't want to be visible within the group as a professional — I felt very strongly that we should all take equal responsibility for the piece. So began my ever increasing verbal silence with the group. Late, I began to feel silenced. I felt more like a representative of all the women who weren't there. And going to prison was the crunch point when all my frustration of not being able to speak or articulate what I felt became clear. As a Greenham woman I had a choice to go to prison. The other women inside did not. I had the support of the group and women outside, and it was time to face my guilt and grow. Coming back was good like the Lion in the Wizard of Oz. I had found my courage and the poem I had struggled to write emerged.

My position within the script is still silent excepting the poem, but no longer in opposition, more in terms of being able to embrace our political and personal differences and respecting our different areas of growth, and that shone through to the audience. Performing in the church was an accident but right. The atmosphere drew together all the strands, creating a delicate, sensitive, and transient pattern. I still have reservations of a theatrical nature about the actual performance, but it was really an extraordinary and wonderful piece to be involved with — quite unique and never to be repeated.

Carmel Caddell

I didn't realise what I was getting into. I hung back a lot, thinking I could join in later, which I did. But it was difficult to take on my share of the responsibility for the play when it came to it.

I looked to Zouffi, Tanya and Tracy as the 'professionals'. I didn't feel so upset or involved in the power-struggles I observed within the group.

I knew after a while that I should be doing something more, but was uncertain about my contribution. I started to feel nervous about it. I got most upset when Zouffi was ignored by Tanya and Tracy on her last day with us. I cursed myself afterwards that I hadn't spoken out in that last moment when they stood there — when it was dawning on me that they were actually going to leave without saying goodbye to her.

After that, at the Christmas break, I felt I couldn't contribute with the play. I decided that I couldn't bear to see them again. I couldn't get over it. I was ill and felt depressed. I realised I would have to overcome my negative feelings about returning to the group after New Year, because the prospect of us not getting the play together made me feel even more depressed than facing them.

I was afraid and deeply mistrustful — somehow Fiona had hung in there, so I would, too. I was alarmed the next time when she wasn't there and I was alone with Tracy and Tanya. I wanted to discuss with them what had happened with Zouffi, but I was too afraid. I let the opportunity go, telling myself that vague references showed their regret. (Well, Tanya had said she felt bad about it.) But Tracy said nothing and she seemed so distant. I carried on, trying to put the mistrust I felt out of my mind. When Sally and Fiona and Max were there as well, I felt better. I was quite relieved when Tracy took her break. It made it easier for me.

I knew it was important for Common Ground to come up with a play. I realised I was not coming out at all, not really. At times we seemed close and then, other times, I doubted if I could like or trust any of the women. Except Fiona. I felt safe around her. I thought 'Whatever she thinks of me, I trust her.' Gradually I noticed Max coming out and challenging Tanya and Tracy, then I started getting the dreams and, thanks to Max, I actually told Tanya the dream I had had about her. This was a big step. Then I sent a card to Tracy — another big step. I was suddenly afraid that she was seriously depressed, and I knew I had to expose myself to her — at least to make an effort. I'd had a flash of her death and was only forced by this to break the fence between us.

These two steps and the rice fast and my dreams helped me have the courage to come out from behind my fence and take my part in the play. If I could have escaped all that pain of self-exposure, I would have — but I knew it would only lead to worse pain if I didn't go through with it.

We all seemed to get stronger. We were saying what we felt. We all began to interact more evenly. I looked forward to the workshops instead of dreading them, and noticed how each of us seemed to have our own struggles.

I didn't come out soon enough, but by the end, I became so involved that I could show my anger with Sally (for reminding me of what I was/had until recently been like — i.e. always looking to Tanya for a lead). I have a link with each woman now. I feel 'real' with each woman. It's been an important experience for me, doing this with Common Ground. In many ways, we hardly know each other, and there is a long way to go in trust. But we held on together and created strong links between each other — something that makes me feel hopeful and happy — as far as it goes.

Fiona Wood
I haven't wanted to write anything about our journey together through these months of working with the theatre group. However, here I am many months after the performance, the night before the script goes to the publishers! I have spent the evening with Tanya and Lily, her daughter, and left, script in hand. It is three o'clock in the morning and I'm on picket duty at the South London Hospital for Women. And I find myself reading the script for the first time — strange to see it on paper. It brings back memories of months spent with six women — Wapping, Riverside and Rotherhithe — always within sight of Old Mother Thames — good times, good spaces.

We do not yet have the skills to construct Remember Rooms, as they do in the Wanderground. Writing seems a clumsy way to reproduce all the emotions, conflicts, creations of a past time. Until very recently, I have neither written nor read anything since coming to Greenham two years ago. Ideas changed daily, hourly, between conversations, confrontations — theory was built piecemeal, moulded through the different perceptions of each woman, fixed long enough to get us through the next action, and as soon added to and changed again. I understand the curse of our grandmothers on he who came to collect the ballads they knew as living, changing sounds — that these songs, stories would die as soon as he wrote them down.

But at some point during these months of working with each other, we decided to fix, freeze our experience together. And having committed ourselves to a date for performance, the show went ahead. And I, who had been petrified to get up in front of six women on our first meeting together to improvise on the theme of that fear, found six months later I actually enjoyed showing off in front of sixty women! From that first meeting, I remember six pairs of arms throwing me back out there again and again. Their applause for me at the end seemed to me then less to do with anything I had created out there, than something they had constructed from it in their own imaginations. Maybe that is theatre! Leave plenty of spaces!

We worked hard on articulating our fences and defences for six months. We played games and talked together and got to know each other very well. For me some of the most important work was done before we went up to the rehearsal room — talking together over coffee for an hour or more — exchanging gossip and experience.

It was very difficult for me during these months to take time off for these meetings — taking time away from Greenham work, I felt very uneasy and divided in myself. It all seemed so urgent — women in crises, actions to be covered, leaflets to prepare, visits to prison, meetings, dish-washing, feeding, talking, listening. I was usually late for meetings, but once there I knew it was important enough to give it everything.

It took many more months after the performance to draw away again. Now I am seeking other ways to create what seemed to me always the most important aspect of our work then — creating a space for us to come in from a man's world to be together as women. To get on with living — to come through what Jill called the period of mourning since Cruise arrived — to acknowledge their power of total annihilation — knowing also they can't take away from us the power we have to go on living, supporting each other with that knowledge. To acknowledge the struggles of sisters for whom the holocaust has already arrived — women in struggle in Ireland, in Central America, women in the Pacific, women in prison, women in famine. For me in the play the prison scene was that acknowledgement — to women on the Front Line.

Wherever we are the struggle for our own space seems paramount — taking down fences in this horrific man's world to make room for ourselves — creating places of healing, sharing childcare, housing, reclaiming the night, learning skills that have always belonged to men — carpentry, building, mechanics — and perfecting our own. To remain centered as a woman is to walk the water like the Newbury witch — between having to face uncomprehending brutality on the one hand and numbing invisibility on the other. Centuries later we are still walking that water.

Who are the witches?
Where do they come from?
Maybe your great-great-grandmother was one.
Witches are old wise women they say.
There's a lot of witch in every woman today.